WHAT I MEANT TO SAY

A PURPOSE PROGRAM MASTERPIECE

DR. CINDY BAILEY
&
THE DAUGHTERS OF ZION

This book is a spiritual reference book, based on actual experiences and life stories of the publisher and the women incarcerated at the South Fulton County Annex facility. To include original artwork, poems, and life stories with copyright permission only for this book.

The chapter "The Conversion Process" consists of articles listed below that were written by authors with copyright permission verified with research and discovered via author website, Facebook, Google search, and BibleGateway.

Rebellion Quote by: Roy Masters, Author of "Hypnotic States of Americans"
June 20, 2012 NewsWithViews.com

I Am Kept Woman - the unknown artist
Woman To Woman Encouragement - author unknown
You Fall - author unknown
Just Be Yourself - Lucy Swindol
Who God Uses -Tracey Fletcher
I AM - bible study research tools
The U in Jesus - Charleen Coleman
Jesus Our Perfect Hope - Charles Stanley
God Said No - Claudia Minden Weisz
© 1980, Claudia Minden Weisz. http://www.andgodsaidno.com

What To Do When You Don't Feel Like Praying - Dr. Carol
Ministries
Pray This Prayer Even If You Don't Feel Like It-
Touchingthesoul.blogspot.com, 2008.
Lord Heal Me - Godfruits.tv
Dear God - Prayer for Healing-Crosswalk.com
Believe God is There for You - author unknown
Twelve Steps of Wholeness - author unknown
Whatever- www.facebook.com/PaulPrabha
This is the Day the Lord has Made Prayer - author unknown
Lord, I Thank You Prayer - author unknown
Those Who Achieve - author unknown

Portions of the lyrics from One Day at a Time - Songwriters: KRIS
KRISTOFFERSON / MARIJOHN WILKIN One Day at a Time lyrics ©
Sony/ATV Songs LLC, Buck Wilkin Music LLC, Buckhorn Music
Publishing Co., BUCKHORN MUSIC PUBLISHERS INC

Artist: Lynda Randle, Album: God On The Mountain, Released: 2005,
Genre: Christian/Gospel

Bedford Hills Prison Information from: Bedford Hills Correctional
Facility for Women - Wikipedia https://en.wikipedia.org/wiki/
Bedford_Hills_Correctional_Facility...

Scripture references: https://www.biblegateway.com

Chapter 3: Word Release- https://www.thefreedictionary.com/release

Chapter 6: Bishop T. D Jakes: "Don't Confuse Talent with Purpose.
www.aol.video clip Oprah's Life Class

Chapter 6: https://www.mindtools.com/pages/article/smart-goals.htm

Consciously Exploring My Purpose - By: Dr. Winsome Miller-Rowe
(Winmil) June 2014

WHAT I MEANT TO SAY...

Be encouraged, be determined, be victorious! We tend to see failures, shortcomings, and obstacles as setbacks, but often, they are really setting us up for our next victory.

So, the next time you are faced with difficulties, seek God and trust that He will work it out!

"And we know that in all things God works for the good of those who love him, who have been called according to his purpose." Romans 8:28 NIV

Captain Tyna Taylor – South Fulton County Annex

Giants do fall. Strongholds are very powerful tools used by the devil to keep us bound in a certain type of thinking, lifestyle, behavior, or even in a relationship. Satan's goal is to steal, kill, and destroy. He will use whatever means to accomplish his goals, and it all starts with deceiving the mind. Satan knows that if he can control our thoughts, our actions will eventually line up and follow what we think.

But the good news is that we are already more than conquerors. The good news is that greater is He that is in us than he that is in the world. The good news is that Jesus has already conquered death, hell, and the grave. The good news is that Jesus took the authority He won over the devil and gave it to...*Us*! Because of Christ's victory over the devil, we have victory over the devil also. Because of this, we can walk in the victory Christ obtained for us and use the weapons Christ gave us to pull down and destroy the strongholds which seek to keep us bound. No matter what particular stronghold or strongholds you may be facing, realize and walk in the knowledge that because you are in Christ, you are already victorious. With prayer, patience, and faith put into action, no matter how long you may have battled a stronghold, with God on your side, you are victorious. Walk in your victory from this day forward!

Written by Minister Tayo Popoola - Purpose Program Facilitator

Table of Contents

Preface

"What I Meant To Say..." There is so much to say in this book regarding my brokenness, my wounded soul, and my healing process. The life conversion of my Saul bka "SiSi" (street name) from my Paul experience developed my kingdom purpose; now Dr. Bailey (my Ambassador name). The journey to identify my biblical characteristics as an APD - Apostolic Petrine Disciple, having a Paul experience may be appalling to some, while others will relate if they are being transparent with our individual shortcomings and flaws.

I was living a worldly life that transparently had strongholds that were REAL, RAW, and UNCUT before moving to a spiritual place of PRAYER, PRAISE, and POWER; Holy Ghost Power.

I take nothing for granted, and never no glory! I am not edifying sin nor justifying the path of pain and brokenness. I want everyone reading this to know that 'life is so short.' We can't keep holding on to the scars and bruises of our past. The pain and hurt from our family generation (known and unknown).

My Jonah journey truly opened my eyes to these facts and the reality that I am not my own. I made it and so will you. When you live and act in an emotional state, you cause more pain and affliction than the original emotion intended to cause. If you're not careful of this emotion and don't recognize its motive, it will destroy your present life and cause damage to your immediate future.

Dr. Cindy Bailey, MS, DMin
Purpose Program - Director of Operations
K I N International Ministry Inc. - Founder

Dedication

To my PAST,

Wow, you really took me on a journey of blindness, disobedience, destruction, and depression. You had me in the mental state of oppression, in the emotion of abandonment, with a heart of anger and in the will of rebellion. You set me up for failure and dangled the worldly vices and strongholds of drugs, alcohol, lying, and promiscuity. You created a daily energy of revenge, deceit, and greed that would target anyone. There was no favoritism or respect of persons when it came to my actions. You then allowed me to be beat, abused, and manipulated by men, beginning with my own child's father. The battle scars are still visible and although you meant for me to die… I still live.

You were so deliberate to destroy my purpose, to steal my future, and kill my anointing, that you led me to prison. You separated me from my family, my children, my ambitions, and my freedom. What you meant for evil, God turned it around for my good! If it had not been for you, PAST, God couldn't use me for HIS purpose today. So "What I Meant To Say!" is, I forgive you. I forgive myself and ask anyone that I hurt during this process for forgiveness. If it had not been for the LORD on my side while you, PAST, set me up for the mess up, I wouldn't be who I am today! So, thank you!

To the Daughters of Zion, who are the women in the Purpose Program at the South Fulton County Annex,

Thank you for allowing me to believe in each of you. Together, we discovered that the three things you thought were unique about yourselves were identical to your top three spiritual gifts God the Father in heaven placed inside of you before any of you were in your mother's womb. Together, we journey and walk in your purpose for the kingdom and God's glory. Crying with you, laughing with you, sharing with you, and growing with you helped me, a wounded healer, purge of all my brokenness residue and achieve a Joseph anointing of forgiveness: to forgive, to love, and to bless. Thank you for those that shared your poems, drawings, letters, and art to be included in this book. Our stories will be a blessing to each reader and a beginning to restoration for all women incarcerated. You women are phenomenal! You women are the remnants in the new centennial movement to draw all men unto Christ! You women are heirs of the Most High God! Therefore, each of you are: Amazing, Anointed, Beautiful, Strong, Talented, Victorious, Wealthy, and Wise!

To God the Father and the Lord Jesus Christ, THANK YOU! Your word is true, and your promises are always fulfilled. In you Lord, we can do everything, and our purpose will never be withheld from any on us. Job 42:2

Acknowledgements

Thank you, former Sergeant Helga Bryant for being obedient to God, having a heart for these women with a vision that created the Purpose Program.

Thank you, Captain Glanton for allowing the Purpose Program to come to the South Fulton County Annex.

Thank you, Sheriff Ted Jackson & Lieutenant Edwards for always giving accolades to the Purpose Program at every Chaplaincy meeting.

Thank you, Captain Taylor for welcoming me and the facilitators of the Purpose Program to the South Fulton County Annex. You always do whatever you can to make sure every security measure is in place and every need is met to have an effective and efficient Bible Study throughout the week.

Thank you, Lieutenant (Holiday), Sergeants (Jones, Adams, Johnson), Deputies (Coolie, Bailey, Crowder, Dias), and so many other officers not individually mentioned. To Ms. Knox and the Nursing Staff, your kindness and edifying spirits will never be forgotten.

Thank you, Minister Tayo Papoola and Minister Diahanna John-Baptiste for your tireless voluntarily efforts and your weekly commitment to come teach the women at the South Fulton County

Annex. Instilling hope and breaking down strongholds. God bless you both abundantly.

Thank you, K I N International Ministry Inc. Board Members and Directors of the Purpose Program for always supporting the vision and having a heart for kingdom building.

Thank you, Dr. Gloria Holden Scott for your prayers, support, and partnership as our accredited bible college for any of the women seeking a degree in Christendom. You are an amazing Woman of God and Spiritual Mother!

Introduction

——————❦——————

What I Meant To Say...

Father God,

I Thank You Lord, that you are my refuge and my fortress and in YOU I trust. I had no spiritual relationship with You to even believe that it was possible that I, a sinner, could be saved by your grace. That I truly dwelt in the secret place of You, the Most High God, and in You, I am sincerely safe while abiding under your shadow, the Almighty!

Oh, how you kept me, Lord! How you delivered me from the Father of Lies and the snare of my enemies. How you kept me from myself (flesh) as I learned to seek You for myself in order to fulfill the plans that You have for me. For this I say, THANK YOU!

Psalm 91 Amplified Bible (AMP)

He (Cindy) who [a]dwells in the shelter of the Most High
Will remain secure *and* rest in the shadow of the Almighty [whose power no enemy can withstand].
2
I (Cindy) will say of the Lord, "He is my (Cindy's) refuge and my (Cindy's) fortress,
My God, in whom I (Cindy) trust [with great confidence, and on whom I rely]!"

3

For He will save you (Cindy) from the trap of the fowler,
And from the deadly pestilence.

4

He will cover you (Cindy) *and* completely protect you (Cindy) with His pinions,
And under His wings you (Cindy) will find refuge;
His faithfulness is a shield and a wall.

5

You (Cindy) will not be afraid of the terror of night,
Nor of the arrow that flies by day,

6

Nor of the pestilence that stalks in darkness,
Nor of the destruction (sudden death) that lays waste at noon.

7

A thousand may fall at your (Cindy's) side
And ten thousand at your (Cindy's) right hand,
But danger will not come near you (Cindy).

8

You (Cindy) will only [be a spectator as you] look on with your (Cindy's) eyes
And witness the [divine] repayment of the wicked [as you watch safely from the shelter of the Most High].

9

Because you (Cindy) have made the Lord, [who is] my refuge,
Even the Most High, your (Cindy's) dwelling place,

10

No evil will befall you (Cindy),
Nor will any plague come near your (Cindy's) tent.

11

For He will command His angels in regard to you (Cindy),

To protect *and* defend *and* guard you (Cindy) in all your ways [of obedience and service].
12

They will lift you (Cindy) up in their hands,
So that you (Cindy) do not [even] strike your foot against a stone.
13

You (Cindy) will tread upon the lion and cobra;
The young lion and the serpent you (Cindy) will trample underfoot.
14

"Because he (Cindy) set his love on Me, therefore I will save him (Cindy);
I will set him (Cindy) [securely] on high, because he (Cindy) knows My name [he confidently trusts and relies on Me, knowing I will never abandon him (Cindy), no, never].
15

"He (Cindy) will call upon Me, and I will answer him (Cindy);
I will be with him(Cindy) in trouble;
I will rescue him (Cindy) and honor him (Cindy).
16

"With a long life I will satisfy him (Cindy)
And I will let him (Cindy) see My salvation."
Amen!

A MESSAGE FROM THE VISIONARY

In respect to the Women at South Fulton Annex-

Maybe you have fallen into a circumstance to which obtaining a dream was not enough and mismanagement of gifts and talents left you isolated. Considering where you have come to be, you may have lost sight of who you are, feel you have lost something you may never have again or are yet holding onto something that you cannot free yourself from. If this is a feeling that is familiar to you, I remind you to have faith. Have faith in who you were, who you are, and who you are destined to be. Have faith in the process, have faith in the journey, and have faith that what is meant to be will be. Have Faith? Have Faith!

A Dream Tree...

In a plight,
In captivity of the mind,
Acknowledging that season's change only with time,
Enduring the valley, of trial and error, Not being able to release certain unique energies of aspirations in thought,
Longing for a family,
That complete image,
Of having to hold, through sickness and in health,
Suddenly, I saw you and felt enlarged, like a star in the sky, I knew someone had then,
Twinkled my eye, But then soon I realized...
Heaven must be dropping a cry.
captured my mentality of reality and wrought a dream.
Suddenly inspired, because all along I knew I had a reason to go on, jumping out of bed embracing the day, for I am now seeing myself as an achiever of better assets having to come in play.
Who would have thought, this dream is out of
Let's see, ambitions to necessitate, acquire, and crave. Which allows one to believe and hope for what they see, an insight of concept, and liberation from reality?
A dream that brought sunshine, acknowledging that season's change only with time,
Patience within me to allow me time to forgive myself,
Patience beyond me to allot you time to forgive you,
Even if my dream lasted for a short period of time.
Just like a tree, it never ceases to reach.
Spreading its branches, being fruitful and multiplying,
Allowing each in every leaf to prosper and weave.
Standing strong with firmness in its own foundation, rooted in grounded beyond all normal surface levels.
For up above its own height is acknowledges the sky,
Still yet standing tall, enduring seasons of all natural humankind.
Just like a tree, never ceasing to reach.
For what's up above,
We cannot always see,
A dream tree,
Aspiring...
O, little me.
Written by – Former Fulton County Sheriff Sergeant H. Bryant   & Purpose Program Founder

CHAPTER 1

Dr. Bailey's Story

I was in 1979 in the Lawnside County Court House in Lawnside, NJ. I surrendered myself with my grandmother's guidance, to appear on a runaway charge. I stood before a judge, and it was then that I discovered I was adopted. To be perfectly transparent, the thought of being abandoned activated an emotion of rebellion that began the spiral downfall of my life. "Why wasn't I good enough for my parents?" Neither of them, my father nor my mother wanted me.

After 16 years of living with who I thought was my father, he would drink, and in a stupor, would constantly tell me that I would "never be nothing" and that I was "not of his kin and would be no good." I then listened to my mother tell him, "Stop saying that to that child, you ruthless SOB - son of a black sheep!" Yep, I now knew why I felt like the black sheep. I now knew why I was subjected to his verbal and emotional abuse and that it wasn't just the alcohol, it was his heart. My adoptive mother had lost a little girl at delivery and this had taken a heavy toll on her and my adoptive father. It was at that moment that another pain afflicted my heart. I didn't know the identity of my biological parents. It was like I had survived and my parents died at my birth. But what I didn't know was why my parents didn't want to keep Me?

Expediently, the enemy took over in the battlefield of my mind, set wretchedness in my heart, and activated my resentful demeanor. I wasn't good for anything, my own parents abandoned me. I would be nothing because I don't even know who I came from. I have no history. My own parents didn't love me, so why should I expect anything more from anyone else? What was the purpose of living a prominent life and continuing my valedictorian education? Yes, despite the verbal and emotional abuse, I was the only child; smart, spoiled, and well cared for, yet it all vanished in the courtroom on that day.

Let me tell you something about rebellion! Roy Masters, Author of Hypnotic States of Americans states it best. He says,

"Rebellion arises against cruel authority, but behind such authority stands hypocrisy. The real sinners are not the rebels but those who drive them to rebellion—the wolves in sheep's clothing: cruel parents, teachers, preachers, bureaucrats, and the downright criminals hiding behind the cloaks of station and legality.

Rebellion can never free you so long as strong emotion is involved, simply because the emotion which converts your discernment of the injustice before you into a judgment of it, causes you then to become secretly subject to the injustice. The hostility that accompanies your judgment transfers to you the character and behavioral disorders of those against whom you would rebel. For example, when you resent (judge) another's judgment of you, in the process you become like the one who judged you: judgmental. Being judgmental then prevents your effectively rebelling. You cannot correct the system because you are reflecting it—beginning to be what you were rebelling against. Hostility causes you to struggle between the no-win choices of rebellion and conformity.

As you fail to affect the system for good and as it affects you for ill, your pride, your ego, feels your failure. It steps in and tries to counteract the effect inside you with more emotion, of hate or "love." That only complicates your dilemma. Your ego does not want to see that you are like those you despise. Refusing to face this truth, by denying facts and rationalizing, you are now rebelling against the truth in your mind. Again, resentment is at work. The same thing is happening in you that you despise in others."

This was indeed the truth. I despised my biological parents for not wanting me. I was very angry with my adoptive parents for not telling me sooner in life. I was tricked by my adoptive grandmother for making me turn myself in to the courts to learn of this truth, this pain, this anger, this resentment, this rebellion. I despised life and anything it had to offer. I wanted revenge. I instantly became Saul bka SiSi!

Let me introduce you to SiSi!

SiSi means *yes* in Spanish. I wanted to do things that pleased me now. I didn't care about rules, regulations, principles, standards, not any of the guidelines or methods that promote integrity and help build character. It was a hustle game of revenge and pleasure now. You get yours and I get mine. A young gangster living the fast life in the world, yet completely broken on the inside. Little did I know, I was a wounded soul. On that day of court, I learned that my biological mother was from Trinidad in the West Indies (which explained my adoptive grandmother's witchcraft and roots). My father was a Cuban soldier on tour passing through. Even if that is true, I haven't yet seen a birth certificate with my father's name on it, only my mother's, Mary Betts. So, I began fulfilling the life of being partly Cuban. This ancestry thing was told in bits and pieces by the only people that would tell me the truth, Ruth and Diane, who would later die and abandon me too; my upside-down journey takes off. Yes, first my adoptive grandmother Ruth, whom I was to her like Naomi was to Ruth in the Bible (although roles reversed biblically), and then my adoptive mother Diane, whom shortly suffers a stroke and is now in heaven. I began indulging in the Puerto Rican lifestyle on the west side of Buffalo, NY where I was known as SiSi, a Mulatto. A mulatto was a mixed breed on the streets, and word was out that I was new to the life but I had it going on! I was beautifully young, intelligent but rude, rough and rachet. I converted to a hustler to the extreme, a drug dealer then addict, promiscuous home wrecker then adulteress, a cunning conversationalist and a master at manipulation. I was a hand grenade set to self-destruct all at once! I loved my life of not having to care about anyone's feelings and emotions, and lastly, their thoughts about me.

The Deal Breaker

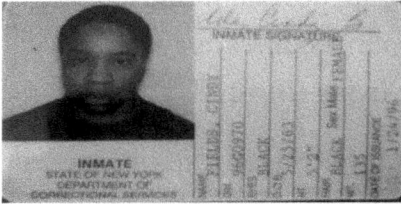

Fast-forward, this rebellion led to my prison incarceration. I had a booking number. I was now an inmate, looked upon as a waste to the taxpayers' dollars and a menace to society!

I lived at Bedford Hills Correctional Facility for Women, located in the Town of Bedford, Westchester County, New York, United States, at 247 Harris Road. Bedford Hills is the only New York State Department of Correctional Services women's maximum-security prison and the largest women's prison in New York State. This prison has hosted many infamous prisoners.

I ran this Saul-Jonah journey of disobedience and self-destruction for nearly ten years. After a plethora of run-ins with the law and criminal misdemeanor incidents, I finally did it big. I was facing twenty-five years to life for possession of a controlled substance with intent to sell. I was leaving behind my son and daughter with the only parents I had, the parents that I had hurt with my cruel words, which I spewed out in the court room. I wouldn't see my children now for twenty-five years! I would be well into my fifties and they would be grown with children of their own, my precious grandchildren.

Lord, please let this cup pass from me! Let me see my children again. I promise to turn my life around for You and I will go back behind the walls, the highways, and the hedges; to the temples of Zion down to Lo-debar and tell of your goodness and your grace! I will decree to a dying world about a living Christ!

Can someone say with me, But GOD! I received a six-month drug program for first time felony offenders and because it was obvious from my criminal activity, I had a drug problem amongst many other issues. Well, it actually ended up being a year and a half term, because I broke the rules. I was being stripped and purged of all bitterness, brokenness, and most of all, myself. I eventually did my time and successfully finished a one to three-year parole bid. The details of this part of my life will be in my life story book, but this book is intended to share the process of healing from brokenness. How to release by writing. How to learn your gifting and purpose. How to say what you meant to say in letters, short stories and poems generated behind the walls. The shedding of my flesh to relationship in the spirit. This is my Saul to Paul; my SiSi to Dr Bailey transition. These are real, genuine works written to express my feelings at the time the poem or letter was written. Works of remorse and love, as I went through my process of GOD remolding me, transformed me into my true purpose. Please enjoy!

CHAPTER 2

The Conversion Process

The Doors Clang!

My first day at Bedford Hills Penitentiary, I read this on the wall! Author Unknown.

Days turn to nights and nights into weeks. And as time passes by, you'll be stuck in routine. Until that one day you realize it's not what it seems.

You'll question your life, your existence, and means.

What is the purpose in all that's encountered; the things that cause grins or forms tears.

Why do we have to be mentally stretched; by our sadness, our hoys and our fears.

How are we meant to spend our whole lives, which path are we to take?

What is 'right', what is 'wrong'? So many decisions to make.

I guess in the end you must follow your heart and do what makes you feel content.

Express your emotions and show how you feel, before your days are all spent.

In my cell, I sat daily thinking about my days turned into nights into weeks! I could still hear the gavel and see the judge's face, ready to sentence me to 25 years to life. The tears of gratitude roll down my face. A flash of my life darts quickly across my face, and I hear a voice remind me about a vow!

Now, we all know we get biblical knowledge when we get in trouble, especially when you get incarcerated. It's just like going to church, to the building all your life but having no relationship. I discovered a relationship with God, My Father behind the walls!

I picked up my bible and immediately opened to: Numbers 30:1-2

Then Moses spoke to the heads of the tribes concerning the children of Israel, saying, "This is the thing which the Lord has commanded: 2 If a man makes a vow to the Lord, or swears an oath to bind himself by some agreement, he shall not break his word; he shall do according to all that proceeds out of his mouth.

Don't barter with God! "IF you do this Lord, this time, I will do this! God doesn't forget!

God constantly brought these things to my remembrance as I was beginning my spiritual walk with HIM. Strangely enough, the first of every month, sometimes twice a month, if there was a holiday during my entire bid, I would always find an article of encouragement and inspiration under my cell. I would ask each of the jail wardens on every shift daily if they knew where the article or prayer had come from, but no one would affirm the delivery. I knew then that GOD had assigned me an angel even while incarcerated. I knew then that GOD still had better for Me. I had hope to become a better person and not a menace or dreg to society anymore. I repented! I was truly sorry and wanted to say it to everyone I hurt, especially my children. I saved these articles over the twenty-three years and read them over and over again in the order my angel delivered them to me. It wasn't until this book that I actually researched the authors in order to share with you! Notice the pattern of the articles that my angel delivered. Every message ministered to the path of my journey of fulfillment in Christ.

Who AM I?

<u>I AM A "KEPT" WOMAN</u>

You see, there were a few times when I thought I would lose my mind, but GOD kept me sane. (Isaiah 26:3)

There were times when I thought I could go no longer, but the LORD kept me moving. (Gen 28:15)

At times, I've wanted to lash out at those whom I felt had done me wrong, but the HOLY GHOST kept my mouth shut. (Psa. 13)

Sometimes, I think the money just isn't enough, but GOD has helped me to keep the lights on, the water on, the car paid, the house paid, etc. (Matt. 6: 25-34)

When I thought I would fall, HE kept me up. When I thought I was weak, HE kept me strong!

(1 Pet 5:7, Matt 11:28-30)

I could go on and on and on, but I'm sure you hear me! Praise the Lord! I'm blessed to be "KEPT."

If you know GOD has KEPT YOU… Open up your mouth and give HIM your praise!

WOMAN TO WOMAN ENCOURAGEMENT

Someone will always be prettier. They will always be smarter. Their house will be bigger. They will drive a better car. Their children will do better in school and their husband will fix more things around the house.

So, let it go, and love you and your circumstances. Think about it. The prettiest woman in the world can have hell in her heart. And the most highly favored woman on your job may be unable to have children. And the richest woman you know… she's got the car, the house, the clothes and just might be lonely.

The word of God says, "If I have not Love, I am nothing!" 1 Corinthians 13

So, again, Love You! Love who you are right now and let God be your barometer. Mirror HIM! Look in the mirror in the morning and see how much of God you see. He's the only standard, and even when you come up short; he will not leave you or forsake you. Smile and let God continue to bless you.

YOU FALL...

"You fall, you rise, you make mistakes, you live, you learn.

You're human, not perfect. You've been hurt, but you're alive.

Think of what a precious privilege it is to be alive... to breathe, to think, to enjoy, and to chase the things of love.

Sometimes there is sadness in our journey, but there is also lots of beauty.

We must keep putting one foot in front of the other even when we hurt, for we will never know what is waiting for us just around the bend.

JUST BE YOURSELF

Sometimes the hardest thing in life is being ourselves. **We so want to be somebody else.** For years I sang with the Dallas Opera chorus, playing the part of other people. It was great; I wore wigs, corsets, fake eyelashes, heavy makeup, and costumes in order to become a waitress, a nun, a dancer, or a lady in waiting. Whatever was called for, I became that. Interestingly, even my friends in the chorus used to say to me, "My favorite thing about all this is that **I don't have to be me."**

The next time that you stand in front of a mirror and want to scream, try to remember that GOD made that face, that smile, those big eyes, crooked teeth, and chubby cheeks. You are his creation, called to reflect HIM. Spiritual transformation does not come from a diet program, a bottle, a makeover, or mask. **It comes from an intimate relationship with the Savior.** Because of HIS nature, HE looks beyond our snaggle-tooth grin and all our faults and appreciates us for who we really are and provides our needs. So, we too can appreciate us for who we really are.

Scripture references: Genesis 1: 26-27; Psalm 139:14; Ephesians 2: 8-10

THIS IS THE DAY THE LORD HAS MADE

God has kept me here for a reason. I survived because HE has a plan for Me.

All my bad relationships, the consequences, the hard times, the sad times, the death of my loved ones, the backstabbing from my friends, the negative thoughts, and the lack of support; I made it because I am blessed!

I release and let go of all past hurts, misunderstandings, and grudges because I am abundantly blessed! I recognize them as the illusions they are, and sent from the enemy to kill my spirit, steal my joy, and destroy my faith; For God is all there is. All else is a lie!

So NOW, give yourself a hug, wipe your tears away, and walk in victory!!! I love you, but more appropriately, God loves you BEST! Be blessed and know that you are at one with the SPIRIT of the LIVING GOD! The will of GOD will never take you where the GRACE of GOD will not protect you!

So may the Lord keep watch between you and me when we are away from each other. Genesis 31:49

"When people show you who they are, believe them the first time." Maya Angelou

WHO GOD USES

GOD, grant me the Serenity to accept the people I cannot change, the Courage to change the one I can, and the Wisdom to know it's me.

The next time you feel like GOD can't use you, just remember...

Noah was a drunk

Abraham was too old

Isaac was a daydreamer

Jacob was a liar

Leah was ugly

Joseph was abused

Moses had a stuttering problem

Gideon was afraid

Samson had long hair and was a womanizer

Rahab was a prostitute

Jeremiah and Timothy were too young

David had an affair and was a murderer

Elijah was suicidal

Isaiah preached naked

Jonah ran from GOD

Naomi was a widow

Job went bankrupt

John the Baptist ate bugs

Peter denied Christ (3X's)

The Disciples fell asleep while praying

Martha worried about everything

The Samaritan woman was divorced, more than once

Zacchaeus was too small

Paul was too religious

Timothy had an ulcer

Lazarus was dead!

Now! No more excuses! God can use you to your full potential. You aren't the message; you are just the messenger.

I AM

Beautiful	Ecclesiastes 3: 11-14
Victorious	Romans 8: 37-39
Enough	2 Corinthians 12:9
Created	Genesis 1: 27-31
	Isaiah 43: 7
Strong	Philippians 4:13
Amazing	Psalm 139:14
	Ephesians 2:10
Capable	Mark 10:27
	1 Peter 2:9
Chosen	1 Thessalonians 1:4
	1 Corinthians 6: 19-20
Never Alone	Matthew 28:20
	Isaiah 54:17
Always Loved	Romans 8: 31

ONE DAY AT A TIME

I am only human. I am just a woman. Help me believe in all I can be and all that I am.

Show me the stairway, I have to climb. Then Lord, for my sake teach me to take one day at a time.

One day at a time sweet Jesus, that's all I'm asking of You!

Just give me the strength to do every day what I have to do. For yesterday's gone sweet Jesus and tomorrow may never be mine. So, help me I pray to show me the way one day at a time.

Lord, do you remember when you walked among men? Well, Jesus you know you're looking below and it's worse now than then. Their pushing and shoving crowding my mind. Oh, Lord for my sake teach me to take one day at a time. One day at a time sweet Jesus, that's all I am asking of You. Just give me the strength to do every day, what I have to do. For yesterday's gone sweet Jesus and tomorrow may never be mine.

So, help me, I pray to show me the way one day at a time. Lord, help me I pray, show me the way. One day at a time.

Whose AM I?

THE U IN JESUS

Before U were thought of or time begun, GOD even stuck U in the name of His Son.

And each time U pray, you'll see it's true, you can't spell JesUs and not include U.

You're a pretty big part of His wonderful name, for U, He was born; that's why He came.

And His great love for U is the reason He died. It even takes U to spell crucified.

Isn't it thrilling and splendidly grand, He rose from the dead, with U in His plan.

The stones split away, the gold trumpet blew, and this word resurrection is spelled with a U.

When JesUs left earth at His upward ascension, He felt there was one thing He just had to mention.

"Go into the world and tell them it's true, That I love them all, Just like I love U.

So many great people are spelled with a U, Don't they have a right to know JesUs too?

It all depends now on what U will do, He'd like them to know, But it all starts with U.

GOD SAID, NO!

I asked God to take away my habit. God said, NO. It is not for me to take away, but for you to give it up.

I asked God to make my handicap child whole. God said, NO. His spirit is whole, his body is only temporary.

I asked God to grant me patience. God said, NO. Patience is a by-product of tribulations; it isn't granted, it is learned.

I asked God to give me happiness. God said, NO. I give you blessings; happiness is up to you.

I asked God to spare me pain. God said, NO. Suffering draws you apart from worldly cares and brings you closer to me.

I asked God to make my spirit grow. God said NO. You must grow on your own! But I will prune you to make you fruitful.

I asked God for all things that I might enjoy life. God said, NO. I will give you life, so that you may enjoy all things.

I ask God to help me LOVE others, as much as HE Loves me. God said, Ahhh, finally you have the idea!

"To the world you might be one person, but to one person you just might be the world.

WHATEVER!

Whatever your trial, GOD sees.

Whatever your struggle, GOD knows.

Whatever your cry, GOD hears.

Whatever your difficulty, GOD cares.

Whatever your problem, GOD understands.

Whatever your need, GOD provides!

Talk To Me, Lord!

Now, I felt a shift inside of me. I felt a release of a remorseful spirit leave my mind and soothe my heart. I stopped crying myself to sleep every night in my cell. Now, I wanted to LIVE and not DIE! I wanted to learn to talk to God and hear from HIM! I wanted to talk to HIM with no interruptions and see God show up for me like HE did before the judge that was ready to send me up the river for life. I needed more of that kind of spiritual power and divine connection.

I got on my knees and began talking to GOD asking HIM to give me HIS direct contact information. I needed an urgent private conversation speaking HIS language. I wanted HIM to even call me sometimes. I needed God's undivided attention, knowing everyone going through something wanted the same from HIM. Of course, I knew about prayer, but I wanted the 'effectual' prayer of the righteous that availed much! The next morning, I started receiving articles about prayer! My angel was at work again.

JESUS, OUR PERFECT HOPE

This is how the LORD responds: "If you return to me, I will restore you so you can continue to serve me. If you speak good words rather than worthless ones, you will be my spokesman. You must influence them; do not let them influence you! Jeremiah 15:19 NLT

Something unique happens when people undergo trials. They are broken in spirit... they come to a place where they're confronted with their own inadequacy, sin, and self-will. Then, in total desperation, stripped of all their devices and contingency plans, they look to God and recognize their complete dependence upon HIM.

Have you come to such a place? Then realize that a person who has been broken has a greater potential to serve God with superior authority, fruitfulness, and productivity than even the most talented person who has never experienced that level of humble dependence upon HIM. This is because the by-products of brokenness are spiritual growth, sensitivity, and godly character.

So today, take heart in the fact that the God who calls you by name is in complete control of your circumstances, and HE has your best interests at heart, even in the places where you feel broken. He is fitting you for HIS service. Therefore, even if you cannot see HIS loving hand guiding you or evidence of spiritual growth, let the trial you're facing have its perfect work in your life

Pray: Jesus, I trust You to grow me spiritually. Thank you for training me for Your purpose! Amen.

That night....

There was a strange noise, and I became very restless this night. I actually sat up in the middle of my bunk! I heard an inmate screaming and hollering that she wanted to die! She didn't want to live anymore! I put my face to the bars to try and distinguish whose voice was pleading for help and what cell she was in. The more I listened as the warden officers rushed running up the cell block, the voice was clearer and then confirmed, it was my new 'jail buddy' friend. I yelled to the top of my lungs, "Hold on and pray! God loves you and so do I!" I saw her face as they passed my cell to escort her to the suicide watch. I called her by her name and she stopped and looked at me with large, sad eyes and a look of lost hope. "Please, know that God has it all under control. God loves you so much as do I. I promise you things are going to work out for your good!"

What had I just promised a human being that was about to take their life? Immediately, I had to talk to God and reassure HE heard what I said to my friend and HE back up and make good of what I said, please! I began praying and crying, walking back and forth in my cell! Not caring if my cellmate woke up or not; at this critical time, I hope she already knew how to pray and would just join in and not disrupt my flow of assignment. It wasn't until I had choked to catch my breath, that I felt a peace in my stomach! I opened my eyes and saw a ray of light and heard a voice say, "It's already done!" I climbed in my bunk and slept like a queen. The next day, cells opened for breakfast, and I saw my friend back on the block. I ran down to hug her and sit to eat breakfast. While saying my grace, I added a "Thank You Lord for having my back!" I started reading more about prayer at the law library. Dr. Carol Ministries wrote this: What To Do When You Don't Feel Like Praying.'

1. ***Don't confuse prayer with performance.*** *Prayer has little if anything to do with King James English pious phrases said with a super-spiritual-sounding voice with one's eyes closed. Tears, dance, song, silence – all may be just as much prayer in the appropriate circumstances.*

2. ***Be real with God.*** *When you don't feel like the "normal" prayers, that may be the very time to just let your emotions flood out in God's presence. Frustration, anger, pain, fear, confusion, excitement – who better to understand you than Him?*

3. ***Choose to listen.*** *Sometimes you may be too tired or angry to hear much right away. Consciously choose to keep*

coming back into God's presence, perhaps after some rest or time. He will speak to you in some way.

4. ***Read other prayers.*** *Sometimes one of the best ways to express yourself in prayer is to read one of the Psalms. Most of them are prayers, and they express a wide variety of emotions and thoughts. Read through a few and see if one doesn't say something of how you feel. Or try another classic book of prayers.*

5. ***If it's quick, it's still prayer.*** *"I'm tired. Goodnight." "I'm stressed. Come with me please!" "Why?" "Help me!" Those are very real prayers. What's important is that you direct them to God – the One big enough to handle it all.*

So, you may not feel like kneeling down or raising your arms and having a happy conversation with God. But you can still pray!

This was so empowering to me. I began finding more scriptures in the bible that spoke about prayer. I fell in love with the book of Psalms because it seemed to have a prayer for everything. I wanted to become whole like David! I wanted God to create in me a clean heart! I wanted to not be double minded but trust God and lean not on my own understanding in all my ways. My angel was at work again! The next articles I received all had to do with prayer. God was molding me to be one of His prayer warriors to stand on the front line!

PRAYER

Prayer is the answer to every problem in life. It puts us in tune with divine wisdom, which knows how to adjust everything perfectly. So often we do not pray in certain situations because from our standpoint, the outlook is hopeless. But nothing is impossible with God. Nothing is so entangled that it cannot be remedied; no human relationship is too strained for God to bring about reconciliation and understanding; no habit is so deep-rooted that it cannot be overcome, no one is so weak that he cannot be made strong. No one is so ill that he cannot be healed; no mind is so dull that it cannot be made brilliant. Whatever the need, if we trust GOD, HE will supply it.

If anything is causing worry or anxiety, let us stop rehearsing the difficulty and trust God for healing, love, and power.

PRAY THIS PRAYER EVEN IF YOU DON'T FEEL LIKE IT!

Dear Lord,

I thank You for this day. I thank You for my being able to see and to hear this morning. I'm blessed because You are a forgiving God and an understanding God. You have done so much for me and You keep on blessing me. Forgive me this day for everything I have done, said, or thought that was not pleasing to you. I ask now for Your forgiveness.

Please, keep me safe from all danger and harm. Help me to start this day with a new attitude and plenty of gratitude. Let me make the best of each and every day to clear my mind so that I can hear from You. Please, broaden my mind so that I can accept all things. Let me not whine and whimper over things I have no control over.

And prayer is the best response when I'm pushed beyond my limits. I know that when I can't pray, You listen to my heart.

Continue to use me to do Your will. Continue to bless me that I may be a blessing to others. Keep me strong that I may help the weak. Keep me uplifted so that I may have words of encouragement for others. I pray for those that are lost and can't find their way. I pray for those that are misjudged and misunderstood. I pray for those who don't know You intimately.

I pray for those that don't believe. But I thank you that I believe. I believe that you God change people and you God change things. I pray for all my sisters and brothers. For each and every family member in their households.

I pray for peace, love, and joy in their homes that they are out of debt and all their needs are met. I pray that every eye that reads this knows there is no problem, circumstance, or situation greater than You, God the Father!

Every battle is in Your hands for You to fight. I pray that these words be received into the hearts of every eye that sees it. God, I love you and I need you to always be in my heart, please!

LORD, HEAL ME!

Lord Jesus, heal me.

Heal my memory.

Heal my heart.

Heal my emotions.

Heal my spirit.

Heal my body.

Heal my soul.

Heal me from whatever separates me from You. Amen!

DEAR GOD

Dear GOD,

Enlighten what is dark in me.

Strengthen what is weak in me.

Mend what is broken in me.

Bind what is bruised in me.

Heal what is sick in me.

Straighten what is crooked in me.

Revive whatever peace and love that has died in me.

Damn, Did I Really Do That?

I can't begin to tell you how embarrassed I am. I had been known as a role model inmate these past few months until this day. The devil is ALWAYS on his job. Don't be fooled into thinking that all the more you pray; the devils will go away! No, they don't go away. They truly become pissed and angrier that you want to change your ways to live righteous. But God sets a standard before your enemy that he never qualifies to meet. The real problem is the flesh, the carnal man! To pray like David and become whole, healthy, and healed requires fasting with that praying. The praying becomes effective when your heart is pure, your mind is stayed on Jesus, and when your flesh is under submission!

My flesh had a way to go. I didn't recognize that I still had anger, bitterness, and unforgiveness spirits that still needed to be purged from my mind, body, and soul. My mindset was, I was reading my bible and praying, so I was healed of all my dilemmas and was just waiting to go home. Well, it all came in full circle when I went off, just snapped out of nowhere on my cellmate. God had given me hints and signs days ago, but I just chose to neglect them because it wasn't pleasing to me. My cellmate always got mail, and I hadn't. My cellmate always had visits, and I didn't. My cellmate was sweet and humble, but I still had a reputation to uphold, SiSi. Prior, during a bible study, we learned about acting like a lukewarm Christian. Yep, I became one of them. I wanted God and the worldly things too. Some say it's, *having my cake and eating it too*! Truth: You can play church, but you can't play God!

So, here I sit in lockdown for seven days for fighting. This was the longest seven days ever! I couldn't eat at all. I would just wake up, take a shower, and go back to sleep hoping the days would go by faster, but it didn't. Those nights, God literally called me and spoke to me. I even felt the presence of my angel in the cell. God reminded me of my David prayer and said, "Release it and let it go!" Let go of the abandonment. Let go of the anger. Let go of the bitterness. Let go of the abuse. Let go of the deceit. Let go of all and everything that's not pleasing to HIM, because HE sees your heart. It was in that cell, I learned to fast and pray. Early in the morning before breakfast count, a male officer came to my cell and told me to get up and pack my things, I was going back to population. But I was only on day five of my lockdown.

My cellmate had been shipped further upstate to do her bid, so I never got a chance to apologize to her, but I promised I would send her a letter that would include an apology. That night, I went to the COGIC bible study, and coincidently, they taught the twelve steps to wholeness, something unique that had everyone in awe, that I am sharing with each of you below. This was the genuine beginning of my purification process. Not only did I receive the twelve steps for wholeness, my angel dropped off a reference prayer to believe GOD is there for you, which I prayed the rest of that month to break the strongholds in my life.

LORD, I THANK YOU!

I am not going to wait until I see results or receive rewards, I am thanking you right now!

I am not going to wait until I feel better or things look better, I am thanking you right now!

I am not going to wait until people say they are sorry or until they stop talking about me, I am thanking you right now!

I am not going to wait until the pain in my body disappears, I am thanking you right now!

I am not going to wait until my financial situation improves, I am thanking you right now!

I am not going to wait until the children are asleep and house is quiet, I am thanking you right now!

I am not going to wait until I get promoted at work or until I get the job, I am going to thank you right now!

I am not going to wait until I understand every experience in my life that has caused me pain or grief, I am going to thank you right now!

I am not going to wait until the journey gets easier or the challenges are removed, I am thanking you right now!

I am thanking you because I am alive! I am thanking you because I made it through this day's difficulties.

I am thanking you because I have walked around the obstacles. I am thanking you because I have the ability and the opportunity to do more and to do better.

I am thanking you because my destiny is not dead! I am thanking you because Father, you have not given up on Me!

In Jesus name, Amen!

BELIEVE, GOD IS THERE FOR YOU!

YOU SAY	GOD SAYS	BIBLE VERSES
You say: "It's impossible"	God says: All things are possible	Luke 18:27
You say: "I'm too tired"	God says: I will give you rest	Mat.11:28-30
You say: "Nobody really loves me"	God says: I love you	John 3:16 & John 3:34
You say: "I can't go on"	God says: My grace is sufficient	II Corinthians 12:9 & Psalm 91:15
You say: "I can't figure things out"	God says: I will direct your steps	Proverbs 3:5-6
You say: "I can't do it"	God says: You can do all things	Philippians 4:13
You say: "I'm not able"	God says: I am able	II Corinthians 9:8
You say: "It's not worth it"	God says: It will be worth it	Roman 8:2
You say: "I can't forgive myself"	God says: I Forgive you	I John 1:9 & Romans 8:1
You say: "I can't manage"	God says: I will supply all your needs	Philippians 4:19
You say: "I'm afraid"	God says: I have not given you a spirit of fear	II Timothy 1:7

You say: "I'm always worried	God says: Cast all your cares on ME	I Peter 5:7 and frustrated"
You say: "I don't have enough faith"	God says: I've given everyone a measure of faith	Romans 12:3
You say: "I'm not smart enough"	God says: I give you wisdom	I Corinthians 1:30
You say: "I feel all alone"	God says: I will never leave you or forsake you	Hebrews 13:5

TWELVE STEPS TO WHOLENESS\

1. Admitting Our Powerlessness
I now see that I, of myself am powerless, unable to control (manage) my life by myself.

Rom. 7 & 8   Rom. 7:18, 19   Rom. 3:9-10, 23   Ps. 32:3-7

2. Trusting in a Higher Power
I now realize that my Creator, God the Father, Son, and Holy Spirit, can restore me to wholeness in Christ.

Ps. 27:4-5   Ezek. 36:27   Mark 10:26-27   Rom. 8:9

Phil. 2:13

3. Centering in God
I now make a conscience decision to turn my entire will and life over to the care and direction of Jesus Christ as Teacher, Healer, Savior, and Lord.

Josh. 1:8-9	Jer. 29:11-14	Jer. 32:27	John 10:30
John 14:6	Matt. 28:18,20b	Mark 10:27	

4. Knowing Ourselves

Having made this decision, I now obey God's call in Scripture to make a fearless, ethical, moral, and scriptural inventory of my entire life in order to uncover all sins, mistakes, and character defects, and to make a written list of every item uncovered.

Ps. 139:23-24	Lam. 3:40	Jer. 23:24	Rom. 8:26-27

5. Admitting Our Wrongs

After completing this inventory, I now will "walk in the light, as He is in the light" by admitting to myself, God, and to at least one other person in Christ the exact nature of these wrongs.

1 John 1:7	Ephes. 5:13, 14	Ps. 119:9-11	1 Tim. 1:15
Acts 13:38-39	Jam. 5:13-16	Heb. 9:14	Acts 2:37, 38

6. Eliminating Character Defects

Having agreed with God about my sinful behavior, I now ask His forgiveness through Christ and openly acknowledge that I am forgiven according to the Scripture.

1 John 1:8, 9	Jam. 4:10	1 John 2:1, 2	Ps. 27:13, 14
Ps. 118:18 then 17			

7. Letting Go, Letting God

I now repent (turn away) from all these behaviors in thought, word, and deed and ask God to remove each besetting sin, through Jesus Christ.

John: 5:14	John 8:10, 11	Job 11:13-19	Ezek. 18:30-32
Rom. 12:1-2	1 John 2:3-6	2 Cor. 10:5	Col. 3:17

8. Making Peace in Relationships
I now make a list of all people I have harmed in thought, word, and deed and a list of all people I believe have harmed me and will make amends to them all.

Eph. 4:29-32	Hos. 11:1-4	Eph. 5:1, 2	Luke 6:31
Matt. 5:43, 44	Matt. 18:15	Lev. 19:17, 18	Mark 12:31
Matt. 5:9			

9. Making Amends and Forgiveness
I now go directly to these people to forgive and to seek forgiveness, reconciliation, restitution, or release whenever and with whomever possible, unless to do so would cause harm.

Matt. 5:23, 24	Isa. 1:18-20

10. Living One Day at a Time
I now consciously and prayerfully continue to "walk in the light" by unceasingly taking personal inventory of all my temptations and sins, and by keeping a constant open relationship with God, myself, and other people.

Matt. 26:41	Jam. 1:13-15	Matt. 6:11-13	Col. 3:13
Prov. 30:8, 9	Eph. 5:15-18	Ps. 4:3-5	Ps.55:22

1 Pet. 5:6, 7   Eph. 4:22-28

11. Meeting God Through Prayer

I now continue in regular Scripture, study, prayer, worship, and fellowship to increase God's will in my life.

Acts. 2:42   Mark 12:28-33   Matt. 6:33   Ps. 89:15

Josh. 1:8   1 Kings 8:56-61   Col. 3:12-17

12. Walking the Walk

Recognizing the impact of God in my life, I now intentionally share these principles and their effect with others as God's Spirit leads and will continue to practice these principles in all areas of my life.

Micah 6:8   Eph. 5:8   Eph. 6:10, 11   Ps. 40:8-10

Gal. 5:1   Rev. 12:11   2 Cor. 3:17

CHAPTER 3

Release & Write

Although, I learned and made it through the twelve steps to wholeness through repetition, I strongly apply step number seven daily; Letting Go & Letting God. I have learned to release it to God by writing it all down. I wanted peace in my spirit, and that's actually how *What I Meant To Say* was birthed. There were things still on the inside I needed to get out and ask forgiveness for or from. However, the chips fell, I had genuinely come to set myself free from the tricks of the enemy playing in the battle fields of my mind.

The definition of the word *release* in Webster dictionary:

a. To set free <u>from</u> confinement or bondage: released the prisoner.

b. To set free from physical restraint or binding; let go: released the balloons; released the brake.

c. To cause or allow to move away or spread from a source or place of confinement: cells that release histamine.

d. To make available for use: released the funds for the project.

2.

a. To set free from obligations, commitments, or debt: released them from their contract.

b. *To relieve of care or suffering:*

When I think of the word release, it brings to memory the scripture, "Who the Son sets free is free indeed." John 8:36 Releasing is the pathway to forgiveness! When we can let things go and trust God to be in control of our lives, we will live a much longer and prosperous life. The poems you are about to read were a part of my release & write. I wrote these while I finished my bid at Lakeview Shock Incarceration Correctional Facility in Brocton, New York. They are not written in any type order but enjoy all of them!

THOSE WHO ACHIEVE

Those who achieve great things are not any smarter or more capable than others. They have simply decided to make use of what's available to them. Those who achieve great things encounter challenges, obstacles, and problems, just as everyone else does. Achievers have simply chosen to work their way through the difficult challenges, rather than be stopped by them. Those who achieve great things experience plenty of setbacks and disappointments. They have simply decided to take renewed determination, instead of discouragement, from those disappointments. Those who achieve great things have exactly the same amount of time available in each day as does everyone else. They have simply committed to making the most of each moment. Those who achieve great things are not any different than anyone else except for this: They decide to do it, and then follow through with persistent, consistent action. In this way, very ordinary people realize quite extraordinary levels of achievement. In this way, you can do it too.

MY TWO FRIENDS

In everyone's life, there are some you grow with and become close.

Unlike your siblings, spouse, or children whose love you give the most.

Well, I've been blessed to have two special friends.

No matter where or what, we'll be a team to no end.

I've given them nicknames; 'Sugar Baby' and 'Boodah Bear.'

We laugh, we talk, we cry, but most of all we share.

We've been in situations causing us to do time.

We've been on adventures, that has prospered our minds.

We've been all cuddled up, crying out our woes.

We've been in our groups sharing war stories,

Laughing at riddles and simple jokes.

We've stuck together like Threes Company

and when things aren't right,

We get together and make peace

Saying our prayers each and every night.

My two friends, I Love them so...

Sugar Baby and Boodah Bear

God Bless You Both!

IS THIS LOVE?

All my life I've been alone,

Persistent and Aggressive

Being the head of my home!

I've met a man and he became my best friend!

I protected my heart and I dare not let him in

The fights, the arguments, and many lies

Just left me sad with swollen teary eyes

The phone would ring and I'd pick it up

His voice full of sorrow and romantic stuff

I would pace the floor and many questions set in

Is this love? When does it start? And how does it end?

Listening to the radio, the love ballads did play

Reminiscing about his comforting and happy cuddling days.

Staring at the pictures, smelling the vase of flowers

Hearing his strong voice whispering as he would hold me for hours.

I walk over to his favorite chair and I hold myself because he's not there.

Again, the questions echo aloud,

Is this love that makes me sad? That makes me smile.

Folklore says, can't live within. I can't live without.

But if he'd knock on the door, I'd jump for joy and shout.

I miss my man; dear Lord so please bring him home.

I feel love growing, all in my bones.

He's on my mind and a yearning heavy in my soul.

Is this love? The answer I truly need to know.

DAYDREAM

I sit on the ground and the sun enriches my hair.

Daydreaming and traveling to a place beyond a care.

The sounds of nature echoes melodies of a beautiful song.

The visions behind closed eyes,

Keep wearing a smile all the days long.

Peace and tranquility are found in every breath

These travels in my mind are indeed a vacation quest.

No pain, No worries, No aches, No tears

If life was a daydream,

Humanity could survive to live a hundred years.

I swam the beaches and oceans; I climb mountains sky high

I've discovered an oasis; I've survived in jungles where many have died.

Sometimes a queen among the rich and famous.

Then an astronaut solving a mystery, in outer space strangest places.

The excitement, the joy, a concert debut.

Then I open my eyes…

Damn, could this daydream be a DeJaVu?

THE MAN IN GRAY

There's a man in gray, that I'd love to seduce.

If I just wasn't a parolee, and the law would turn me loose!

I'd cuddle with him and squeeze him until he was fully mesmerized.

I'd pamper him and love him until his moans were sighs!

From his head to his toe, I'd admire his muscles so broad.

Then when he turned over, I'd make him feel what he did to my heart.

I'd freak him to no end! Send him pleasures with ecstatic loving.

I'd turn exotic and erotic and calm his every neurotic.

This man in gray is so fortunate today. That I am not free, and I am awaiting Boaz to come my way!

GOD IS GOOD

God is good, All the time.

He's a God of His word

There's no doubt in my mind.

He holds true to his abundant promises

Written in the word

Just trust him, believe him,

You'll never go unheard

If it aligns with his will

Then it shall be done!

God is so good

The proof, HE gave his only son.

DEAR LORD

There has finally come a time in my life that I no longer want to suffer or bear strife.

I've always known about 'You' and your divine Son,

How 'You' created the world and HE died to save the wretched ones.

I call you on the main line, all day every day.

I also read your word to maintain and function properly.

I know you're a loving, kind, and merciful God,

Who forgives me for my sins even when I do not.

You protect me from Satan's attacks,

Whether I'm acting like doubting Thomas or Judas Iscariot.

So many times, you've interceded, rescued, and saved a sinner like me.

That this time in my life, I want to truly live for thee.

To act on my faith and trust entirely with my soul,

So, when you come, like a thief in the night,

I'll be waiting and worthy to come home!

Your will be done,

Your Daughter, Cindy!

WHO AM I?

I am flesh on bones; a descendant of Adam & Eve

A carnal minded man, cursed by sin, yet saved by Grace.

Saved by Grace? So how can I …

Have a stinking thinking attitude? A funky body language that smells so 'fleshly'

Was that I who…

Rolled my eyes at my neighbor? Or said, "Tell them, I am not home!"

Or had the judgmental thought, *Wow, what is that she is wearing?*

Or used foul language in a smooth rhythm in my conversation.

Is that me…

Who'll embrace you so reverently in church, yet walk briskly past the Salvation Army donation can?

Who's head of a ministry, but too busy to minister to a stranger?

Who will rob Peter to pay Paul but skip or penny pinch the tithes and offerings basket?

Who wants to be recognized in public events, but can't volunteer to evangelize for the glory of God.

Who am I...

I need to check myself, because I am wrecking myself!

I'll never hear him say, "Well done, my good and faithful servant."

I need to not always, fall short of the glory of God.

I need to recognize I am covered in the flesh that's no good and dying every day.

Yet, I am truly saved by his grace and mercy and the blood of Christ.

It was shed for all men to make the way for us to have eternal life.

It's not about who I am, but who lives in me? Am I really about my Father's business?

I have his anointed gifts birthed inside of me, that makes me rich before great men. I have the Holy Spirit as my GPS, so I am guided and directed at all times.

Let's be genuine Christians, not just on Sundays or when we feel like. That's not WWJD!

Let's live in the spirit as HE lives in US and we can go higher

And deeper in our relationship, salvation, life with Christ for the Kingdom!

THANK YOU, LORD!

There is a God in heaven, this much I know is true.

HE's done so much more for me, than any human can do!

Now that I am no longer blind, I can see the true beauty in me.

Now that I am no longer deaf, I can hear God's voice so tenderly.

These words you read are not thoughts, but true experiences entailed from my heart.

Do what you will with me.

I know where there's pain and suffering, there's also joy in a new beginning.

I also know to praise You, whether it be good or bad

It keeps hope alive, regardless if I'm sad.

Heavenly Father,

I Thank You for your love you always bare

For having grace and mercy, when no one else was there.

For giving your only Son, to save a wretch like me

For coming back again, that I one day may reign in eternity.

Yes, Lord! Have Your way. Make me worthy to be with you,

When you come for your saints, I pray you'll take me too!

Thank You, Jesus! Thank You, Lord!

INGREDIENTS OF MY DREAM COME TRUE

With pen in hand and the wheels turning in my head, I began to create a plan.

In my plan, I added 'will.' I concentrated, I decided and persevered

This dream I'd fulfill!

To nourish 'will' I included 'hope.' I'd be real with myself,

Make a change and believe, I could cope.

With 'will' working and 'hope' alive, I appointed 'faith.'

To supersede as my guide.

Prayers, praises, and sacrifices. Believing - GOD is the truth, the way, and the light.

My dream came true…

I used these ingredients and I worked my plan.

It didn't take a lotto dollar, fortune teller, nor a scam!

REMEMBER THIS!

A word of encouragement. I would like to remind you that you are a very special person.

Even if you may forget it sometimes, I'm here to remind you that you are a very special person.

I have so much faith in you! And I know that you'll be able to do the things you want and need to do in life.

And if you ever need me, I'll be here for you! To cheer you on. To stand by you. To encourage you!

Everything will be just fine, you'll see.

So, this is just a little note for you to keep. Although I can't always be there with you, these words can be.

So, I want you to save this in a special place. That every now and then, you'll think of me.

I want you to set this card aside and remember it when you're feeling wonderful. So you can remind yourself that this is how you make me feel.

I want you to set this aside and save it for the days when things haven't necessarily gone as planned.

Or the clouds are hanging around a little longer than they should and maybe this will help to cheer you up.

When you get home in the days to come and reread this note while sitting on your bed, favorite chair, or in your secret place,

Remember that I'm probably sitting here, as I usually do, smiling too thinking of all the wonderful things about you!

I love you unconditionally! I love you unconditionally as true love does.

I do not wish to judge you or criticize you in any way. I just will let you be you.

No one can change my heart about you, so don't you change your heart about who God made you!

We all fall down, but we get back up! You are worthy and wonderful! Don't ever forget it!

ALL I WANT...

All I want is to Love You, for the rest of my life!

To wake up every morning with you by my side.

Knowing that no matter what happens, I'll be able to come home to your loving arms.

All I want is to share everything with you!

To talk with you about our ideas, our dreams, and the little everyday things.

The things that make us laugh and the not so little things that we can't help worrying about.

All I want is to give you my love as a place you can always come to for acceptance!

Or the simple comfort that silence brings, when things left unspoken can still be understood.

All I want is to grow old with you!

To watch our life unfold and our dreams one by one come true.

All I want is to Love You, Forever!

What I Meant To Say....

To my children that I left in your grandmother's care, I love you both so very much and will always have love for the both of you! Did you know that I loved each of you long before you were born? You were a part of my future when I was created. When I first held each of you in my arms, I knew then my childhood dreams had come true. I remember staring at each of your perfect little features and feeling thrilled at each new sound and expression you made. A fierce need to protect you came over me then, and it has never gone away.

When you both were tiny infants, I was able to hold you close through illness and heartaches. I could hold your hand as you faced new experiences and my presence and guidance seemed to assure you of a certain level of safety. But little by little, I have had to let you go and allow you to make your own decisions and your way of life. So often I wanted to call you both back and have you stay in the protective circle of my arms. I never wanted either of you to have to face injury or heartache, yet I knew that you would in order to grow strong and trust GOD. I can't explain the things that happen in our lives. I surely can't but if I could, I would try to make sense of all the things that are happening to you and show you all the great things that are going to happen real soon. If I could, I'd turn all those worries and pains into smiles. The smiles right now that make everything alright and the way you would want it to be. That's how much I care and love you. I may not always have the right words for you. I may not always do the right things by you or for you. I may not always know the right answers for you, but I will always be here for you.

Now you are all grown up and making your own decisions often facing life alone. Just remember that no matter what, I love you! I could never stop loving you. You are the hugs and smiles from the past and the hopes and dreams of my future. Take care my Son and Daughter and know that you are never alone. We are forever connected by the strongest bond there is: The love between a mother and her child.

Love Always, Mommy Cindy

CHAPTER 4

Meet the Daughters of Zion

How It All Began

This section of the book actually began April 6th, 2019. The first day I was called to Chaplain duty at the South Fulton County Annex. Just for clarity, I am not an employee of the South Fulton County Annex facility nor an employee of the South Fulton County Law Enforcement.

I am a trained and certified volunteer Chaplain for South Fulton County Law Enforcement and now volunteer Chaplain at the South Fulton County Annex.

The day I drove to Union City to meet former Sergeant Helga Bryant to pray because the shortness of staff caused some duress and lots of tension. We know the effectual prayer of the righteous availed much but when two or three come together, HE is in the midst! But that wasn't the real reason I was called to come there. It was to fulfill the vow I shared with you back in Chapter 2. The scripture in Numbers 30:1-2 reads:

Then Moses spoke to the heads of the tribes concerning the children of Israel, saying, "This is the thing which the Lord has commanded: 2 If a man makes a vow to the Lord, or swears an oath to bind himself by some agreement, he shall not break his word; he shall do according to all that proceeds out of his mouth.

*Don't barter with God! "IF you do this Lord, this time, I will do this! God doesn't forget! *

God remembered the vow I made to HIM. It would be twenty-three years today that I am free from a twenty-five to life sentence. It was HIS perfect timing to still find me worthy to fulfill my promise and orchestrate it with the vision HE gave to another willing vessel, former Sergeant Helga Bryant. God told me that these women were HIS Daughters of Zion! He would use these mighty remnants to proclaim the word of God before HIS second coming. Although it began in I-Pod where I met my first amazing group of daughters (I love each one as such), I've now had the joy of being with all the women in A, D, E, F & G Pods.

Ladies, you give me life! Each of you have touched my heart in a very special way. You bring smiles to my face! I cover you all in prayer and have so many other prayer warriors praying over you also. I believe in each of you because you all are so gifted, beautiful, anointed, wise, and able to do all things through Christ that gives you strength.

Don't let the grave rob you of your wealth by dying and burying your visions and dreams with you. I hope this book encourages

ALL of you to use your gifts to fulfill your purpose for God's kingdom and live a righteous life of abundance and overflow!

The poems and letters you are about to read are the original works of the author. Nothing has been changed or altered for publishing. A waiver and release have been signed by each author with the understanding that all proceeds go to the Purpose Program to build transitional housing, support groups, and assist with education and other rehabilitation needs.

WE Have Talents & Skills

WOW! WOW! WOW! Yes, each of you are astounding! Your works and talents are astonishing! Thank you for contributing your great works for other people to read and admonish all across the world! Thank you for believing in yourselves! Thank you for being committed to the Purpose Program and intentionally wanting to change your lives, transform your mind, and live in God's will and bask in HIS favor! Thank you for always being transparent in class and purging all of your past bottled up emotions! God is not done with any of you yet!

THE DEMON INSIDE

The demon I hide was part of my Pride,

The demon IN ME, who I thought I need.

It's clearly sent signs, that clouded my mind,

The demon of depression, the demon disguise

The demon I hide was part of my pride.

The demon in me push souls to the side.

But I the one with light decides to fight!

I won back my pride like I won a prize.

My demon defeat redeemed him beneath

Now I clearly see signs. I took over my mind.

So it's just a phase when you are feeling weak.

The battle is won, no demon I seek.

I strengthen myself, got back my soul

And I am Me again, I am whole!

Written by Latavia Austin

HOW GOD CAME TO ME

My name is Cyndi Andrews. I am an inmate at the South Fulton County Jail. I lost my dad three years ago now. I have been struggling with a drug addiction ever since. God came to me this past January 2019, while incarcerated in Jackson County, Ga detention center. I was arrested for driving on a suspended license. I was only arrested for 7 day. I was placed in a cell by myself. I noticed I was in a room with just me. I noticed all the other room's where piling up. I wasn't sick when I came to the jail, but at meal calls, I never experienced anything like this. I just couldn't chew my food. I just didn't like the way it felt in my mouth. The texture was nasty, so I quickly spit it out. I am normally always hungry especially in jail. I can't wait for the next meal, or who is going to put money on my account to eat. I pushed the plate away and thought to myself, at least I can lose some weight.

Day three before lights out before nine pm. I heard a voice say, 'you're fasting.' I means in jail, who ever thinks about fasting, right? I mean in jail; we are always thinking about being bonded out. I knew this was the Holy Spirit! I quickly thought back to my mom. I didn't know about fasting. I remember asking my mom, why do you fast? She answered, 'some demons you can't get rid of till you fast and you pray a lot.' I thought to myself, I'm gonna see what this is all about. I went to sleep that night praying. I knew I prayed all night long. I talked with the Holy Spirit all night long, because before I knew it, the lights for breakfast call at six am the next morning was coming on. I felt as if I never slept at all. I said to myself, well I'm still in jail, so I'm going to sleep all day. I couldn't remember what all I prayed for. I just knew my brain went all night long. HE also gave me a dream. I then knew how the world was going to end.

The Sun. The Holy Spirit told me I as a chosen one. The Holy Spirit was with me like picking up the telephone and talking. Asking anything and instantly getting an answer. I was released after seven days. I seen so many prayers answered and thing happening all around me. I remember saying, "Wow, I prayed for that." When things happened, I said I must have prayed for that one too or I prayed for that person. I didn't eat for seven days. I had so much energy after being released and not eating for those seven days. I know this, it was the most amazing experience I have ever had in my life. I don't know how much longer I could of went without food. I ate two chicken strips from Zaxby's after being released. I know my appetite didn't come back for two months. I had so much knowledge and energy it was amazing grace. I knew if I continued to get high and be in the mix with the wrong crowd, the Holy Spirit, I thought would give up on me.

I am here to get clean. I am ready to be released sober minded. I have a calling on my life. I had to be sober cause, HE told me too. I am ready to see what HE has in store for me to do next. I can't wait for the blessings in store for me as well. HE said, "Are you waiting?" I want to tell you so much more. I know this, GOD is real! Living the rest of your life knowing something is different instead of wondering what if. I ask may the Holy Spirit be with You and everyone who reads this. Believe and watch now, what HE can and will do in your life. The two keys in life are understanding and love. You have to understand someone to love them. You have to love everyone! God Bless You All!

Written by Cyndi Andrews

PURPOSE

My purpose is to maintain focus and get my life together for myself as well as for my family (love ones.) To stop being in denial about a lot of things. By doing that I need to start looking at what I do wrong and stop accusing everyone for my wrongdoing. Jail is included.

I see myself looking pass being incarcerated so I can get my art and design established in a worldwide nation. So my goal is to sat in God's hands, work on my purpose from now on so in the next years, maybe in months to be what I always dreamed of being and put my mind into it and see where it can lead me.

My negative purpose was my downfall, but it can be turned into a positive purpose where it can uplift me in every way. Seeing my family hurt makes me want to try as well as strangers helping me does nothing but pushes me forward. I understand now that it's a reason and purpose for everything. This is a lesson learned. You know you are somebody, if a person you don't know or barely knew comes in your world to acknowledge, that your somebody besides the friends you thought you had.

Written by Artist Lykeria Bailey

LOVE

The love in your heart wasn't put there to stay. Love isn't love until you give it away.

Written by Judy House-Baxter

WHAT I WANTED TO SAY

My story I have to tell is a blessing because it has allowed me to know that there's a God. I was looking away from my mother at 9years old I didn't see my mother till I was 18years old. During the time I was separated from my mom I was I was raped 3 times during that time. I was 13 years old. It was by the preacher of my church. The second time by an unknown stranger at 16 years old, and the last time at 18 with my newborn we were snatched up in the deep of the woods tied up to a tree for a week my newborn on the ground for 7 days. God is good he allowed no hurt, harm, or danger to come my way. A homeless person came and saved us. It was confirmed that there is a God. No matter what you go through in life have faith that God will bring you out. God doesn't give you no more you can bare. God is a good God. He saved me and he will surely save you.

God Bless,

Written by Marie Clemmons

WHAT 'I' MEANT TO SAY!

What 'I' meant to say is...

I want to say a lot, but how can 'I'

When 'I' really want to cry. Screaming, yelling and letting it all out!

What 'I' meant to say is... 'I won't die!

Pacing back and forth, holding my head,

Asking God, "Please, Please!" When God is clearly telling me don't beg!

What 'I' meant to say is...

Here 'I' go again. Look at Me... Weak, mad and sinning in all ways.

Dropping to my knees, just to give GOD praise!

What I meant to say is...

Pressure is hard, tears are flowing. Watch God keep me going!

What I meant to say is...

Written by Cassandra Cobb

MY NEW BEGINNING

I am a woman who gave birth to five children, but never been a mother to them. I am a woman married but never been a wife. I am a drug addict and an alcoholic. I am a woman with regret and a lot of shame. I am a woman who cries out to God for help. I have a problem and need help. I am a woman headed to rehabilitation, in hopes it will help me change my life. Because, I am not happy with living the way I was living. I am no happy with myself or the hurt I have caused my children.

My heart is with God and the family he blessed me with. I hope that by going to rehab, I will be headed towards a bright new beginning and will find purpose and plan for my life. I want to get to a point where my past doesn't define who I am!

Written by Nicole Daniel

BREAK HER FREE

She walks the paths that leads to win wins she's optimistic and elevates from within. She's smooth and oh so damn fly. She's versatile, unique and captures the eye. She's undeniably attractive, alluring and something to be fantasized. We've all had a piece of her essence we can't resist even if we tried but the only only things that keep her away are hate, judgement, strife and all things ungodly or using her in vain. Who is this creative? Where is she? And what is her name? but why do you ask, when you see her every day? Why do you hold her captive restricting her to play, let her loose do NOT keep her bound because the more you lose her, the less she'll be found? You have the key to your hurts and your

67

pains, break free from BONDAGE be freed from your chains. You can save her, right how this day and beauty will meet you right where you are, each morning, each day.

Written by Lasherae Davis

SAME 'OL SONGS

This life is very deep, the roads that lie ahead can be very steep. There's power in the tongue, therefore, be cautious of what we speak. Our days could be long or short, empty or full, blessed or cursed, joyous or cruel, we make the choice. We decide our fate, so let's not complain about the consequences we may have to face.

Build the spirit, nourish the soul, redirect the mind and learn to understand the reflection life has shown in order to obtain a future we must know where we have gone. Otherwise, we're going to find ourselves stuck, hopeless, resentful in the same spot, singing the same 'ol songs.

Written by Lasherae Davis

FOOD FOR THOUGHT

As I Cindia Denis sit in Union City Jail, I'm wondering how I can become apart of Dr. Cindy Bailey & the Daughters of Zion Purpose Program book. The first thing that comes to mind is food for thought. We live in a world where common sense is no longer common. I realize how important it is for us children of God have to start planting seeds of pain common sense.

The enemy comes to kill, steal and destroy but most of us never realize that the battle agains the Devil has already been won! All negative thoughts such as jealousy, envy, worry, fear, bitterness, anger, laziness those are seed the enemy comes to plant inside of us but those seed cannot grow unless we feed them. We become our thoughts. The more we allow negative thought to live within us the bigger they become. We create our own destiny, our feeling rise and wants us to follow but we should guide our feelings instead. When God said to clean the inside of the cup then the outside will be clean, I believe HE was saying we should clean our thought then our actions will follow.

None of us are meant to build God's Empire alone, one can plant seeds, one can wate the seed and even cut and prune. When the weeds begin to grow we can remove them. I also want to add that failure isn't final. Mistakes doesn't have to be stumbling blocks they can be stepping stones. Ashes for beauty!

Written by Cindi Denis

MY SUFFERING

I am suffering with being locked up and not being with my kids. Because I feel like I let them down by being away from them. But when I get out of here, I am going to make sure, I won't be away from them anymore. I can't make up the time that I've been away but what I can do is move forward with them now and keep going with the time I have.

This has made me look at life a whole lot different and when I walk out of these doors, my head is going to be on straight. I'm going to let God guide me the way he wants me to go. I'm going to follow his lead and not my own. I am a better person with a whole new start of life ahead of me. God Bless me and my family! Love Y'all!

Written by Tyra Ealey

CHOICES & DECISIONS

My life just got turned upside down when I met a man that I thought I could trust. Now, I'm sitting in a jail cell thinking where did I go wrong. I think about it time to time. Was it him or was it me or was it the both of us?

I am only twenty-two years old and I've been locked up since July 20th, 2018. I got locked up when I was 21 years old. I had a hard life, and everything was going good until I met this man. I told this man my whole life story. I told him everything about me and I even stayed with his mom when I wasn't staying in a hotel room on Fulton Industrial. Basically, the man I thought was my boyfriend was really manipulating my mind. I was having sex for money for him and I really loved him. No matter what, I really believed everything he told me because, I thought he was telling me the truth. He told me that he would never lie to me. He told me he would make sure that I was straight no matter what. He told me that I was his girl and I believed every word he would tell me. He had my heart in the palm of his hands.

Now, that I have been locked up a year, I have been thinking and asking myself questions like, "Does he even love me?" "Why did he lie to me?" I just want to say to every woman out there, don't let these men use you for sex or money! Play it smart because at the end of the day, there is only one man that will never do you wrong. There is only one man who will treat you like a queen that you are, and his name is God the Father!

Don't ever forget that you are loved unconditionally by HIM no matter what!

Written by Tiara Holmes.

MY TESTIMONY

In college, on a basketball scholarship, everything paid for, my own car, and only eighteen years old. Sounds like life is pretty good huh? How can someone mess up something so good? Well, I did. Currently, I am housed at the South Fulton County Annex, inmate#1808239. I have been in here for nineteen months, with some serious charges and I thought all hope was lost until God sent me an angel who taught me, "But God!"

That angel happens to be Dr. Cindy Bailey. She has taught me my life's purpose and that God has other plans for me other than being in this horrid jail. This message is to all the young females who think there is no hope for them… "But God!" I know what my life isn't over and soon, I will be home and continuing to go to college. I just have to remember, "But God!" He has the last say so and HE will never let you down!

P.S. Choose your friends wisely, because you may end up somewhere you don't want to be!

Written by Naya Michelle Hunter

DR. BAILEY

From the first time I heard you speak and the way your story touched my heart,

I knew it was the start of how I wish to be.

You didn't even know me, So how could you see

Inside my soul so clearly, And the future I seek?

Every week you came, you're a breath of fresh air,

Along with encouragement I need in a place so hard to bare.

The lessons you teach, and bible verses you preach,

Are never lost on me, As I seek to have your peace.

You make everyone see their own 'special' ways

So, they can grow every day, For that I have to say

Thank you for showing the need to pray.

You have given me hope, When its so hard to cope

And when I'm feeling low, I want you to know

Before I let myself fall, It's your words I recall.

You are a rare woman indeed, In a place so in need

Of hearing the story, you tell

You must have gone through hell.

Your powerful words of motivation

Is truly enough to move a nation

Yes, these might be my words but on behalf of us women

I feel you have made us lemonade from a whole bunch of lemons.

I want you to know how much you are appreciated

Cause when god made you an angel was created.

Written by Amanda Jackson

U.C.C. O's

I'm inclined to use my poems for entertainment sometime so please know that no shade is thrown inside this rhyme.

Here is a little flow about the Officers we know.

In the morning we have Hart so we "roll our asses out the bed" to start.

Johnson is a little less harsh on the mic in a nutshell what's not to like.

Please make sure your teeth are straight on the mornings we have Miss Gray.

Mitchell and Brenton never work the east side my feelings are hurt because I don't know why.

73

On 3-11 we have some cool officers you see, even though it appears they are the busiest to me.

Harris makes me laugh everyday cause she always keeps it 1k, slamming doors left and right but always ready for a fight.

Smith doesn't have one hair out of place and make sure you stay out of her face.

Hudson is too cool to be a C.O. she is slick like a friend to us on the low.

Olysse voice is peaceful to the ear, she needs to be on the radio somewhere and I'm being so sincere.

Coleman and Charles are the most patient with us so if there's trouble with them you pushed them too much.

Cooley is the G.O.A.T you see cause she is a Scorpio like Combs and Me!

Moving on to 11-7 overnight all we want is for you to turn off the light.

Greatest of all time,

We have the Echols slinging bread on the trays, she is a breath of fresh air in so many ways.

Don't do the "Catwalk" when Hilton is around or pods B, C or G is where you might be found.

Philpot is always positive showing so much care which is very much needed in a place so hard to bare.

Speller will listen to every word you say but will quickly tell you "go away!"

Torbetis not one of many words but please be believe she'll make sure she is heard. To be real she really slick nice but make sure you "ask for ice."

Cleveland is like a beautiful pearl and I'd be rich if there was a dime for every time she said "mirror."

Please don't try these two because you should really know at any given time they both trained to go.

Crowder you go above and beyond with nail clippers and books even if we are a big bunch of crooks.

Mr. Johnson and E yawl stay with the men in the intake cells cause back here we women are hell.

This poem was for the officers no doubt but for Sgt Johnson, McCray, Pitts and Jones I have to give a shout out.

I hope you enjoy this writing of mine it truly helps me pass by my time.

I know some inmates make it hard on you so from my pen to your eyes I appreciate you!

Written by Amanda Jackson

MOVING FORWARD

So many years I cried

So many tears I cried

Still moving forward

75

I cried so many years

I cried so many tears

Letting go of the grudges

My heart was hardened

Wouldn't budge

The pain

Lived in my veins

Chasing the spirit of my blood

Letting go of the grudge

Being led by the soul

Story still untold

…So many years I cried

So many tears I cried

Still moving forward, I cried

So many years – I cried so many tears.

Written by Tia Johnson

"A LETTER TO MYSELF"

When I was 8 years old my mom left me at home with my stepfather, he rapes me. Stab me in the head with a butcher knife in my head. Shot me two time and stabbed me once in my knee but I am here. Got on drugs at the age of 18. I've did it all but just know God got a plan for me. I could've been dying a long time ago, but he got me here. It's never too late to talk to someone talk it out don't hold it in. I thank God I am doing better.

Written by Aiesha Lovett

A LETTER TO FUTURE SELF!

Dear Future Ms. Kris,

Who would have thought that you would have made it this far? You got your pot of gold at the end of the rainbow only because your reached for the stars. It was never a fairy tale, though at times that's how it seemed. Your faith kept your vision alive and now you are living your dreams. Your son is all grown up finishing college and becoming a doctor. His wife is pregnant, and they are having their first daughter. You are now free, and you will be there when delivery day comes. Not long ago you were always known to be the first one to run. Through hard work, patience and lots of faith, you have finally learned from your mistakes.

You are much wiser and older and now realize what is worth. You did not let your past define your future and therefor you wouldn't change anything for any amount on this earth. I'm proud of you! Stay Blessed, Your Past Kris!

Written by Kristen McDaniel

A BROKEN CHILD

As a child I grew up sheltered. Sheltered from the world as a foster child's baby who couldn't keep me. So, she gave me to the only person who wanted me, my GG! My great grandmother, who was my dad's grandmother. And although she did her best raising me, there were things happening to me that she didn't even know about. It was not because she didn't care but because she was too old to keep up. I was too young to know right from wrong. My family was very tight knit, you would think but really, they just knew how to keep secrets.

Growing up in my great grandmother's house was like any other grannies' house. All the grandkids came there to play every day except what my cousins called playing was having sex with me with all their friends that were all teenagers. All the while, I was five (5) years old. It happened every day all the way up to my tender age of twelve (12) years of age and it happened right under every one's nose. That is when I started to act out. That's the age that I thought having sex would make people love me or like me because that is what I had been taught.

All my life long, I had been taught wrong. I ran away at the age of thirteen (13) years old, only to find out what I thought was love was torture. I was raped repeatedly by people I thought were my friends. I was pimped out, sold and beaten up to the age of sixteen (16) years of age, that's when I discovered cocaine. Cocaine made me feel like I was on the top of the world. It took all my problems away for the moment, especially when I was high. So, my pimp kept me that way, HIGH and I thought that was love. I thought he cared cause rape and abuse was l knew that all started with family.

I held in all this pain. I never told my family why I bailed out and left home, but they never asked me either. Well eventually didn't have to ask because I finally told them after I put myself through rehabilitation and group therap. But like I thought, they didn't care. They blamed me like I knew they would which sent me on a downward spiral. Once again, that's when I met Him. That's what I'll call him to keep his name a secret. He taught me the game. He taught me how to sell drugs and really get money. Once again, I thought that was love. I had been looking for love in all the wrong places all my life and when I thought I found it, I ended up in jail for trafficking a kilo of cocaine, two guns, two pounds of weed and an ounce of methamphetamine.

My life was over, so I thought but God decided to give my another chance, so I ended up on probation for ten (10) years. This is when I decided to get closer to God! I can admit, you can't change in a day even though that's what some people expect. You can't and don't even try it, it's not possible. I'm still a work in progress but I'm only human and I'll never give up on myself and you shouldn't either. It is never to late to change and it may take a while but in the end it will all be worth it because I am a survivor and that's all that matters.

Written by Tacara McLemore

HOW CAN YOU JUDGE ME?

How can you judge me, and you never walked a day in my shoes?

How can you judge me, and you never had to go asleep cold?

Had to be shackled by steel or ever had to eat your food you weren't sure was even food!

How can you judge me, and you never walked a day in my shoes?

How can you judge me without asking me what is in my heart?

Without looking for the truth in my eyes. Without hearing what my heart has to speak.

How can you judge me, and you never walked a day in my shoes?

How can you judge me, and you never been left in the darkness alone or felt the coldness of emotions?

How can you judge me, and I've already been judged!

Written by Glenndria Morris

ONE LIFE LOST, ONE LIFE SAVED

My life of addiction has cause more than enough heartache. Being hooked on crack cocaine for more than sixteen years was the worst thing ever. During those years I've experienced, I've seen and I've dealt with more than most; not saying that there is someone that hasn't faced worse. I'm just saying that I caused myself and others a lot of pain.

I have been incarcerated more times then I even care to count. As a matter of fact, that's where I am today. However, the only difference this time is that I'm here to make a change, a self cnage and a spiritual change. I've learned that this is a generational curse and I'm to break it starting now. I've hurt many but not as much as I've hurt my Father in Heaven, who has given me more chances than someone should be allowed to have.

I've been to prison three times and I still didn't get it. I didn't even learn how to be a better criminal because I just keep ending up in a place where no one really cares. A place where I'm always being told what to do, told what time to eat, time to get up, time to shower, time to go to bed. Let's not even talk about the men I turned to! Boy, I really knew how to pick them, men that were abusive and loved doing drugs more than me. A match made in hell!

By the way, did I tell you that I'm a mother of four? No, I forgot to mention them, just like I often do outside these walls. I seem to always forget that the four beautiful gifts that Yahweh gave to me. I forgot those gifts because I was too busy getting high and chasing broken dreams. Not realizing that my dreams were in front of me all the time, those four precious little ones that my Father gave me.

After sixteen years of prostitution, drug use and countless men, I finally got my awakening. My oldest son was now carrying the torch of our generational curse of incarceration, which was passed down from both my parents to me and now from me to my son. I thank Yahweh everyday that Austin didn't pick up my drug addiction. Austin turned to the streets for family, love and acceptance. He turned to becoming a gang member. He ended up getting locked up on a two year sentence, got out only to be locked back up there weeks later with a five year sentence. I haven't seen my child in over three years and finally got to see him. Yep, I gotto see him, my baby, my first born, when I had to give his spirit back to the Lord. You see, my son was murdered! He was killed after being locked up for two months. I will never again get to kiss his face, dance at his wedding or hold his children, to be a grandmother. I know that the loss of my son's life won't be in vain. He lost his life to save mine and I am going to break this curse by giving my other children the mother they need so they will have a chance.

Written by Amanda Noble

A MESSAGE TO THE MOTHERS

To the women that have kids, please keep them close. They are precious and very loveable! I am sitting in jail for a mistake, but I can admit that I am responsible for some of this. I left my child with a friend and didn't know she had drugs in her house or that she would leave her unattended.

God warned me while I was out dancing to go back to check on her, but I didn't listen! By the time I came back for her, it was too late. Only God knows, that if I was listening, I wouldn't be sitting in jail. Even though I didn't have the drugs, and it wasn't my house, I was still charged. My kids are my everything! God knows I will give my last to be with my kids every day. I will make it through everything I am going through. I know my kids love me with every inch in my body. I was sat down in hear to realize my life had a purpose and that I was going down the wrong path.

HE had to wake me up! To all my young and older mothers, please take pride in your life and your kids. I know being a single Mother is hard. Being persistent with prayer, hard work and with your goals. It's never too late to get your life on the right path and make your dreams come true. Kids are very smart; they know and sense everything. You have to be the most careful person, when it comes to your kids. Be cautious and very overprotective with your life.

Written by Michelle Norris

<u>SINCE A YOUNG CHILD</u>

Since a young child, I've been thru hell and back. I was labeled the bad child because I acted out. I've always been rebellious and hardheaded. Always learned lesson the hard way because I didn't listen. My Mother did the best she could. It was just herm my sister and I but most of my life it was just me and my mom because my sister would come and go. I've always been attracted to the 'bad boys!' I always was pulled into the streets. I've always been told that I'm too pretty to act the way I did, which I didn't understand or care.

I started to be out in the streets hanging around the wrong crowds. I went to the juvenile for the first time when I was fourteen (14) years of age and this started my downward spiral. I've known since I was young that I have a purpose on my life, but I have always just did my own thing. I've currently been incarcerated for a year and this time I've spent has given me time to re-evaluate myself and the direction my life is going into.

I feel like God sat me down to give me time to change my ways and thinking. I think sometimes, I can't handle the things I'm going thru but then I remember that I've been through worse! My whole life I have felt like the failure. Failing my mom, my kids, my family! In 2017, September 18th, I lost my best friend, my kids father. It was from there I felt lost. I moved to Atlanta, on

83

February 2018 and from there I went on another downward spiral. Now, I'm incarcerated, and it feels like I'll never go home. What are you saying to me this time, God?

Written by Daniella Perkins

MY NAME IS SANDY REED

This is my first time here and it has been a wild experience. My name is Sandy Reed and I have a story to tell. Since I have been here in the South Fulton County jail, I have changed mentally & spiritually. I have finished first phase of the Purpose Program because I was moved to New Beginnings Pod.

I learn to open up and talk to people because I was always closed up. I learned to read and do math. I learned to be around a lot of women, and I had to follow rules, that I never really did. Instead of fighting, I walk away.

I have to keep in mind my kids and grandkids and that this is just temporary. I should have thought before reacting. The constant abuse just kept running through my mind and I just snapped! I've got myself into a bad situation, but I know God is working things out for my good!

Written by Sandy Reed

LIFE LESSON

I can't begin to sort within; the heartache and pain my life has been.

Enough to drive a wise man insane!

The struggle, the drain; that it takes to start my day,

To be frank and plain, Put it simple as a grain;

My ups act like a rising crane; knocking down what I've built, the energy, the strain.

These words I use may seem strange, But I keep my distance, yet within my range

In my right mind; far from deranged. My highs, my lows; my battles my woes.

My friends my foes; helpless like a child with a runny nose.

I find a way; I use codes to dodge some of these holes that life sometimes oppose.

I keep faith, I be strong, I find strengths: I hold on. Letting of my wrongs.

I read books; I write songs! I'm gonna make it, the damage is done.

It's never too late, so celebrate!

Written by Mallori Reed

I HAVE BEEN RESCUED NOT ARRESTED!

Fifty-six years old and in jail for the first time in my life. Coming to jail for the first time on some serious charges- murder! I just couldn't believe it. Growing up in a house where I was being molested, raped by my stepfather; being told by my mom that I should have been aborted! Told that little girls who didn't listen needed to be or could be sent to orphanages. I know now that what little part of me that my stepfather didn't destroy, my mother not realizing what she was doing, destroyed the rest of me. I spent years hiding from reality behind sex, drugs and alcohol. Retreating to what I thought was going to save me, I became pregnant by the age of eighteen and put all my faith in a blonde-haired boy, who took me on a forty-year emotional rollercoaster ride. I never felt complete and always felt like I was missing something but dismissed it as me being restless and bored.

I Thought my later years in life would be filled with love, grandchildren, and retirement. It was the life I was supposed to have after raising three kids and being there, being at my husband's beckon call. Then in November of 2017, Satan came in to finish what he had started all those years ago. He definitely came to kill, steal and destroy every fiver of my being: two suicide attempts, my forty year marriage lost to another woman, my house, lost in an ugly divorce war and because, I am sitting in jail, I am no longer allowed to see my grandchildren. My whole world gone, taken from me.

My first day incarcerated I wondered, how will I ever fit in, how will I ever survive? Fitting in; in a place where worldly time stands still. I guess that's why when I look around, people are clinging to the telephones or they are glued to the television, watching the same old reruns over and over. I really don't think anyone was really interested in what was on, they were just trying to escape this jailhouse reality. I remember in the beginning, calling home, every single day as if I were clinging to a life preserver in the middle of the ocean.   Trying to cling to the outside world from behind the walls of a place where time stand still. The longer I was here the more I realized that I was focusing on the wrong things. I opened the Bible, and actually started to use it for something besides a place to store phone numbers. The more I studied the Bible, the less I was trying to cling to the time that was passing me by on the outside. I decided to devote my time to rediscovering myself. I decided to learn why I was here and what did I want tout of the life that God gave me.

I soon realized that God had a plan, a purpose for me. The more time I devoted to the word of God, the clearer my purpose became. I started thinking more about the women God kept putting into my life. Through months of Bible Studies and devotion to my Father, the Lord has led me to become a Minister, a warrior for Christ and to open a home for women, to help them before time ends for them. I received confirmation of God's will for my life in April of 2019, when the Lord brought Dr. Cindy Bailey into my life. From that meeting, God brought in two more blessings into my life: Minister Tao and Minister Baptiste. With the help of these three wonderful ladies, the good Lord has set me on my path, my purpose, the destiny HE had in store for Me. HE has allowed me to see that even though I am incarcerated, I am no longer held by the chains that kept me bound for most of my life. I thank HIM everyday for putting me in a place that saved my life through Christ. I am truly blessed and I am truly a Daughter of Zion! As I close, I am reminded of this passage:

"I pray that the eyes of your heart maybe enlightened in order that you may know the hope to which he has called you, the riches of his glorious inheritance in his holy people." Ephesians 1:18

Written by Petra Reese

PLEASE, DON'T JUDGE ME UNTIL YOU KNOW MY WHOLE STORY.

Growing up was a maze of dysfunction, but as an adult now, I like to say if they knew better, they would've done better. I grew to learn that it's ok, didn't always mean it's ok. That pretty smile wasn't always to show happiness and happiness was a very elusive idea that we could always pretend existed with a pretty smile and an 'it's okay.'

That was the circle and it just continued as long as we were willing. I jumped off the ride shortly after the birth of my second beautiful daughter. Last stop, Atlanta, GA! I decided to do what I thought was better; get my disrupted children and run as far as I could to get away from the rapist & pedophile who preyed on "us." With a young but strong mind, so I thought, I was off in my Ford LTD with the boyfriend of the month.

Less than a year in, we'd all split from that apartment on Cousawattie. I had no plan, but I owned a Buick LeSabre. My life lesson partner provided. So, with now where to go, homeless with two kids, we slept in that Buick. I took us to the truck stop to shower and we lived like we had it. I'm not sure my girls knew but I did! So as a dancer, I would drop my girls off at the sitter, go to work after they ate bathed and slept. I would pick them up in the morning, then dropped them off at school only to find somewhere to park so I could sleep and get back to life after school.

I met my best friend in life, Darryl at a bus stop on Campbellton Rd. Life started changing. I got us a place to live although we did move around a lot as me and my girls grew up. Jazzy T's was the turn up and start to think about permanent situations. T's showed me a lot of fantasy but also a lot of real life! Baby number 3. Life kind of became a speedy blur. Plenty of cars, homes, money, stashes and then came a firm decision. I have to change my thoughts and with those decisions came federal investigation car accident death and federal prison then what felt like rock bottom. Hurry up and get it together before you end up sleeping in one of these cars. Starting over CDL life almost there and a life altering car accident that changes life as we all knew it but we gotta stick together. We're all growing in our separate spaces all together. My adult daughters and my son, who's going down the wrong path. (I think due to the massive changes in our lives.) They need me. (What's in my head pushing me to quit what I started to make our lives better.) Married to a woman (long story) who has now become good for me but not good to me. So, I mentally checked out. God sent a new beginning house man job.

Fast forward to Oct. 23rd, I married Mr. Reid. Happiness overload! Thirteen (13) days later, before I could change my name, I am referred to as Inmate Fox arrested for, I don't know how many shades of murder. After defending myself in a stand your ground, right to retreat situation with a man painted at the worst stop on the west bound train stations at a time when the world was already scared due to the violence of the police and the criminals at night.

Yet, with fast forward again about four (4) years later almost to the day, I find myself back in the moldy Union City jail where Fulton County houses it's female inmates as a convicted murder with a life to five (5) year sentence with an attorney who's not responding to multiple calls from multiple people who failed to tell me he'd never had a jury trial. What I heard was, I took your money and sold you a story that I couldn't do in real life but hey sorry.

People wonder why people have a hard time trusting "the system" because when you've spent your molding years fighting and it's been a consistent fight into your adult life, fighting with things you thought you'd never have to fight with or through again. At some point, everything starts to look like a fight. Now, I'm sitting here ready to fight again until I'm free because no matter what happens, I've won in my life. My father who is in heaven has a different plan for my life. I am just a woman who works hard and tries to live right. I just cracked the curtains so you can peep inside and know me on the surface just a little.

Written by: Mrs. L Nicole Reid

LIVING WILL

C – Communicating through the Holy Spirit.

H – Hosting Peaceful thoughts.

R – Resting in Jesus's name.

I - I am the Great I AM

S - Supplication, Mercy, Grace

T – Thomas became a true believer.

I - Am very thankful for my life, and my children's lives, (God being there.)

A - Amos was famous for Jesus.

N – Name above all names, JESUS CHRIST!

Written by Shantica Riley

Lost & Found

Dew Drops glisten off the trees,

Deep inside your soul I see.

The clouds are tinted a purple hew

Some are pink and some are blue.

Through the wilderness, I come upon

The rushing stream that flows,

And there I see.

A bed of thorns. In the middle a fragrant rose

I sit to listen in stillness,

While I'm waiting for thee.

Suddenly I'm made aware,

Of your voice from out of the sea

In the bible it states,

that he will be coming back soon

Until that moment;

I'll sit & stare at the moon

Written by: Beckie Slaughter

WILLPOWER TO CHOOSE!

Could you please excuse yourself enough to be transparent taking away your other self just enough to be coherent there are lessons that is to be learned yet still some to be taught with many gifts to discern there's a battle that's to be fought whose side do choose to stand up with in battle? Its imperative that we must not lose it's a fine line that we straddle.

Written by: Beckie Slaughter

TIME

I read Dr. Bailey's book 'Acronym Preacher' and I what I wanted to say this to the women incarcerated.

Time is God's time. There is a time for everything. This is, was the time for me to gather my thoughts and to sit and think about what my next step is. It started here in jail again for me. So my next step is to transform. Then my next step is to let go of things and people that gets me caught up if I realize it or not when it's in motion. I must pay attention. Then my next step is to magnify His holy name. My next step is to stay in His word for the rest of eternity (the rest of my life) and don't forget or drift away from it. So I have stopped counting my days I have been here and started my countdown to leave. This time doesn't matter because I am not coming back. My thoughts are exactly like Dr. Bailey's on page 22: It's my time to pray and not to curse. Time to get to know God not for what HE has done but who HE is. Time to make that change like the man in the mirror. Time to create a plan for eternity not destruction. Time to fill myself with God's word (audio, visual, literature, fellowship) and not drugs and alcohol. Time to let God bring an end to emotional and fleshy attachments. Time to be comforted and counseled with God's love not prostitution and fornication. I tell you now is the time for God's favor and now is the day of salvation.

Written by Kendra Yates

CHAPTER 5

Behind the Badge

───────✦❦✦───────

Two Sides to a Story

As a trained and certified Law Enforcement Chaplain, I mentally live the life of an Officer. We study incidents, cases, trauma, and crisis! We have been involved in real life simulations. But the common perspective of an Officer with a badge, it's not what you say to the public citizen about how good you are at policing. It's what the public citizen feels about the police based upon what they see every day. Whether we want to acknowledge this or not, perception is reality to the public citizen.

However, we fail to realize that an Officer of the Law is a human being! He or she is not only getting up every morning to risk their lives, but they have life issues the same as we the public citizens. It's seldom personal and becoming a Law Enforcement Officer is harder than you think.

Many have a relationship with God and a heart for God's people, You and I! Don't be judgmental of anyone, specifically an Officer with a badge. Enjoy the encouraging words from the Officers, because there are two sides to a story. Thank you to each officer, who took time out of their demanding schedule to write an article for this chapter of the book.

IT'S OK

I just wanted to say to all the women that it is okay to get off track sometimes,

that's how we as women become stronger.

The past does not predict the future, there is always time for change.

Always remember somebody is always in a worst place than you and it's only temporary.

Sometimes we have to induce pain and setbacks to see what's in front of us.

It won't be easy but you only fail if you give up.

Self-love is the key, you can get all the advice and tools

But at the end, it's up to you to make a change and believe in yourself.

Push through even when the odds are against you!

This is Officer A. Bailey

South Fulton County Annex.

FORGIVENESS IS FREEDOM

Through so many trials and tribulations you will find that your heart can sometimes become hardened from so much pain you had to endure. But I must encourage you today that operating in forgiveness gives you the freedom you need to have peace. Your peace is depending on you to forgive the wrongs and move aggressively towards brighter days. Remember as it has been said before, forgiveness is for you, so I need for you now to be free and get your peace. It's time!

Captain/Pastor Jackie Gwinn-Villaroel
Unstoppable Praise Ministries

BEHIND THE BADGE

Let me begin by saying **"Behind The Badge"** holds many facets of experiences. Some days are more challenging than others. It can be overwhelming for men but especially women becoming arrested and they enter the doors of incarceration for the very first time, losing their birth name and instantly becoming just a bunch of numbers. During my years of experience working behind the badge, I've seen many women hurt, abused, angry, devastated, fearful, heartbroken, lonely, and disappointed and while many are shamed about it, others have no remorse or regret of becoming a repeat offender. Despite whatever circumstance or situation it may be, God can and will make a way. If he can deliver Paul and Silas from their troubles while in jail, surely He can deliver you.

The Bible says in Proverbs 3:5 Trust in the Lord with all your heart and lean not unto your own understanding, in all your ways acknowledge **HIM** and **HE** will direct your path. It's just that simple. Hold fast to what is true and don't lose hope. Your situation may be temporary, or it can be a very lengthy one, but what I do know is God specializes in things that seem impossible, if you only believe. My everyday walk and talk "Behind The Badge" here at South Annex Women's Jail is to motivate and encourage you that trouble don't last always. So just know you are more than a conqueror, and if God brought you to it only, **HE** will bring you through it.

This is Officer J. Coolie

South Fulton County Annex.

SHE IS MY SOLDIER

She is MY Soldier

Her enemies have engulfed her like a pack of hungry lions

Their Vengeance will never succeed, despite how hard they're trying.

I created this special person, whose honor will not be debated

No one can stand against what I, the Lord, has created

She is My Queen and My child. We will never depart

For I will always keep her close to my heart.

I will not allow her enemies to abuse and scold her

My brothers and sisters, she is My soldier,

Her enemies will smile and think they have succeeded,

But I had already provided her with everything that she needed

They will use their powers to try to attack her

But prior to their vengeance plot, I had already wrapped her

In the blood of the Lamb, to protect her from harm

For I will come running when she sounds the alarm

See, I knew what I was doing when I took time to mold her

She is strong, she is faithful: **She is My soldier**

Beauty is a blessing, but it can also be a curse

Knowledge is power, but it too can bring the worst

She finds herself surrounded by evil and spite,

But she calls on My name daily, and that's what I like

When she calls upon My name, just know she is heard

I always lend a tender ear to her every word

Enemies all around, who will try to control her

But she has honor. She has strength. **She is My soldier**

She always does good things, to keep all peace as they were

But her enemies will take her good and use it against her

Warm spirit and kind heart, that's how she will always be

She will stand steadfast, unmovable, just like a tree

So, come at her, you enemies. Come with all your might

But this one soldier isn't going out without a fight!

But I trust she will do all that I told her

She listens and she cares, **she is My soldier**

See, I prepared her in a special way that no one will understand

I will not leave her to suffer in the hands of man

She will stick to the fight when she is hardest hit

It's when things go wrong, that she will not quit.

Now, she will sit and wait for me to do my work

For she will not be the only one suffering and hurt

I am always here, and my arms are to hold her

To protect her from all enemies, for **she is My soldier.**

They will gather against her and try to pull her down

But all the time they didn't know, they were building her crown

Pray for all those who hurt you, for their time is near

Be strong My child. I got you. Do you hear?

All your pain and suffering have all been noted

Just be sure to take heed to all that I have quoted

Listen enemies. I'm about to fulfill everything that I have shown her

I am her guidance. I am her rock. **She is My soldier**

Written by Officer Louise Crowder, BBA

BE ENCOURAGED

Be encouraged, be determined, be victorious! We tend to see failures, shortcomings, and obstacles as setbacks, but often they are really setting us up for our next victory.

So, the next time you are faced with difficulties, seek God and trust that He will work it out!

"And we know that in all things God works for the good of those who love him, who have been called according to his purpose." Romans 8:28 NIV

Written by Captain Tyna Taylor – South Fulton County Annex

CHAPTER 6

Stay Kept

Know Your Gifts

Remember, your spiritual gifts are not your talents and skills. But the three unique things you know about yourself, God had already created within before you were in the womb! So, operate in your spiritual gifts, knowing they are the grace of God at work within you, empowering you to match your deep passions with the world's deep need. Although the gifts are given to individuals, they are given to build and strengthen community and to meet the needs of those around us. Reflect on these scriptures to perfect your gifts. I Cor 12: 4-5; 1 Peter 4:10; Romans 12: 4-6. Above all remember Proverbs 18:16:

AKJV : A man's gift maketh room for him, and bringeth him before great men.

LEB: The gift of a person will open doors for him, and before the great, it gives him access. TLB: A gift does wonders; it will bring you before men of importance!

MSG: A gift gets attention; it buys the attention of eminent people.

Know Your Purpose

Remember, your purpose is your motivation. It's the reason that something is done, created, or exits. What do you purpose in your heart? God's plan stands firm forever and his purpose will stand. What God intends, what he has in mind, what he pleases, what he purposes and plans, what he desires for your life is God's goal and lines up to HIS will for your life.

Jeremiah 29:11

11 For I know the thoughts that I think toward you, says the Lord, thoughts of peace and not of evil, to give you a future and a hope.

God will carry out his purpose in you! Nothing can thwart God's plan. Nothing can thwart You of your purpose!

Job 42: 2 (AMP)

2 "I know that You can do all things,

And that no thought *or* purpose of Yours can be restrained. Reflect on these scriptures to understand God's purpose for your life. Proverbs 19:21, Psalm 33:11, Ephesians 1: 9-11 & Romans 8: 28-29

Bishop T. D Jakes quoted it best from his message; "Don't Confuse Talent with Purpose"

He says, "A shining talent like dancing or acting is hard to hide, but a true-life purpose can be tougher to identify." Bishop Jakes says that yes, being good at something doesn't mean it's your calling. "You must understand that the purpose is an underlying chemistry that makes you live your life," he says. "I was sitting on a speaker and I said, 'This speaker will bear the weight of my body. It will make a chair in a pinch',," he continues. "But it was not designed to be a chair. I am not using it for its highest and best use."

"Many times we are pushed into functioning in an area that is not our highest and best use because someone needed us to be something we were not created to be. You may start out doing something that was not 'the thing' that you were created to do," says Bishop Jakes. *"It may only be the thing that leads to the thing you were created to do. So don't stop at where you are as if it were the destination, when in fact in reality it may be the transportation that brings you into that thing you were created to do."*

THEN, make sure you have an action plan! God said, to write the vision and make it plain! Habakkuk 2:2 HE also said, a man without a vision will perish! Proverbs 29:18.

➕ Write your goal and what you intend to accomplish!

1) **Goal:**

2) **Results/Accomplishments:**

➕ Make sure your Action Plan consists of:

1) **Purpose:** To create a "script" for your improvement effort and support implementation.

2) **Directions:** Develop a work action plan for each goal identified

3) **Action Steps:** What Will Be Done?

4) **Responsibilities**: Who Will Do It?

5) **Timeline:** By When? (Day/Month)

6) **Resources: (A)** Resources Available

   (B) Resources Needed (financial, human, political & other)

(7). Potential Barriers: (A) What individuals or organizations might resist?

   (B) How?

8) **Communications Plan:** Who is involved?

   What methods?
   How often?

Evidence Of Success *(How will you know that you are making progress? What are your benchmarks?)*

Evaluation Process *(How will you determine that your goal has been reached? What are your measures?)*

Make sure your GOALS follow the S.M.A.R.T guidelines.

Specific: This answers the questions: What will be done? Why is this goal important? How will it be done? and describe the results (end product) of the work to be done. Your goal should be clear because if not, it will cause you to lose focus and not maintain motivation to accomplish it.

Measurable: This answers the question "how will you know it meets expectations?" How do I track my progress? When you know how you are progressing toward your goal, it will keep you focused and motivated to keep you on track.

Achievable: This answers the questions "can the person do it?" "Can the measurable objective be achieved by the person?" "Does he/she have the experience, knowledge, or capability of fulfilling the expectation?" It also answers the question "Can it be done giving the timeframe, opportunity, and resources?" Your goal should be realistic so you can attain it. You must be willing to put in the work, time, and be up for the challenge to achieve.

Relevant: This answers the questions, "should it be done?" "why?" and "what will be the impact?" Is it something you really want to accomplish? What is my objective toward this goal?

Timely: This answers the question, "when will it be done?" It refers to the fact that an objective has end points and check points built into it. Sometimes a task may only have an end point or due date. Sometimes that end point or due date is the actual end of the task, or sometimes the end point of one task is the start point of another.

Finally, Stay in Touch!

Make sure you stay connected with me and your facilitators. Attend our outside support groups. Stay in your word! Stay connected to God in prayer! Join a good bible-based teaching church where you can grow your gifts and fulfill your purpose for the kingdom. Visit the Purpose Program facility soon to be built with the proceeds from this book, grants, and a plethora of philanthropist donations. We speak it into existence, in Jesus name!

CONSCIOUSLY EXPLORING YOUR PURPOSE

I am spirit having a human existence, that, I can clearly see

I am here for a special reason, for there is no other like me

As I evolve, I seek my purpose, and am consciously exploring

With special attention to my talents and where my life is going.

My thoughts are really powerful, so I try to be constructive

This vibrational energy is real and is best when in the affirmative

There is abundance all around me of love and peace and health

Opportunities flourish so I channel them to my wealth.

Wherever I put attention and focus, this produces my reality

So, for my actions and communications I take full responsibility

I give thanks for all my blessings; I find them as I reflect

This attitude of gratitude brings the abundance I expect

I give willingly and it often returns to me tenfold

My love is unconditional, and I believe that's better than Gold

I teach people how I want to be treated and forgive intentionally

I honor my values and attitudes and help others continually

I respect those in authority, to their wisdom I give much value

I show empathy to my peers and give a listening where it's due

I divide my time between work, rest, and play

And plan my priorities in a very special way.

People I meet along my journey may participate someway

But I must consciously decide the part I allow them to play

This way I am being responsible for the life that I create

With guidance from the Master in whom I put my fate.

SO....

Reach for your purpose in life! And take things one step at a time.

Live life carefully. The scene can change in the blink of an eye.

The journey will be tough, Rise to the challenge!

Empower your world and find your balance!

CHAPTER 7

Remember This Always...

NOTE OF ENCOURAGEMENT

If you are going through hell, keep it moving. It is not enough that we do our best; sometimes, we must do what is required."

Dr. Cindy Bailey, I am humbled to have the opportunity to encourage you in the excellent work you are doing with the Women of Purpose Program at South Fulton Union City Annex.

Many women's lives will be changed as this program inspires and empowers them to identify their life purpose and declare it is never too late to rekindle their dreams.

To the women that are sharing your experiences and talents in this book, I encourage you to pay attention to what you are good at and to what you love. Pay attention to what people are saying to you. You may have your purpose right under your nose and not recognize it.

Some thoughts I want to leave with you are:

Always remember God loves and understands you, and He has predestined a **plan** and **purpose** for your life. Now is the time to prepare for what you want in this life for you and your family and to not only do just enough but to do what is required.

Obstacles are a part of life. So, when you experience obstacles or setbacks, you must be able to preserve until something happens. I encourage you to preserve beyond limitations and barriers that are sometimes self-imposed. Sometimes those barriers are mental because you don't believe you can do it.

I applaud you and the life experiences you have shared in this book. Your voice is needed, and there are people ready to share in your future triumphant.

Dr. Gloria Holden-Scott, author

Wounded Soul
God's Provision is in His Purpose
Breaking the Curse of Generational Iniquities
New Beginning, Take Nothing with You
Can you Believe God is Able?
Sister, I am Not Your Enemy

www.gloriaholdenscott.com
www.newbeginningministry.net

CHAPTER 8

The Good Times

THANK YOU, GIFTED DAUGHTERS
OF ZION!

Thank You, Officer Coolie for UCBT!

Certificate of Appreciation

This certificate is awarded to

DR. BAILEY

In Recognition of your support for **UCBT!!**

Union City Basketball Team

AMAZING & INCREDIBLE ART BY:

MY MONROE

By LYKERIA BAILEY

MY JESUS

By SHARVON PETTAWAY

THE JACKSON FAMILY

By SHARVON PETTAWAY

KEEP GOD FIRST

By QUINN SCOTT

THANK YOU FOR SUPPORTING THE PURPOSE PROGRAM!

THE PROCEEDS FROM THIS BOOK WILL BE USED TO BUILD A HOUSING TRANSITIONAL FACILITY. THE FACILITY WILL ENCOMPASS A TWENTY-FOUR MONTH REHABILITATION STRATEGY TO END RECIDIVISM.

WE ARE ALSO SEEKING ANY & ALL SUPPORT OR ASSISTANT TO REHABILITATE (2) HOUSES TO INITIALLY BEGIN 'WE WON'T GO BACK PROJECT."

2020 WE ARE TARGETING TO EXPAND THE MEN'S DIVISION OF THE PURPOSE PROGRAM.

PLEASE, TAKE TIME TO VISIT OUR GROWING WEBSITE: WWW.KININTERNATIONALMINISTRY.ORG

PLEASE, BECOME A PARTNER OR SPONSOR! YOUR DONATIONS ARE TAX DEDUCTIBLE. YOU MAY GIVE @ **$IHAVEKINGDOMPURPOSE** - CASH APP

MAKE CHECKS PAYABLE TO: K I N INTERNATIONAL MINISTRY INC.

C/O PURPOSE PROGRAM
P O BOX 112
DOUGLASVILLE, GA 30133

PLEASE, EMAIL ME OR THE STAFF @: IHAVEKINGDOMPURPOSE@GMAIL.COM

KINGDOM BLESSINGS,
DR. CINDY BAILEY
PURPOSE PROGRAM - DIRECTOR OF OPERATIONS!
4 0 4 - 7 1 7 - 2 8 2 4
#KINGDOMKIDSDOKINGDOMTHINGS

www.ingramcontent.com/pod-product-compliance
Lightning Source LLC
Chambersburg PA
CBHW071133090426
42736CB00012B/2110